"Humor and sarcasm are two characteristics that I hold most dear in a person and Melanie Dale delivers in large quantities. She says the things that we all think but aren't sure we should say out loud and the pay-off is a hilarious, real look at parenthood."

—Melanie Shankle, *New York Times* bestselling author and speaker

"*Calm the H*ck Down* is such a refreshing book that gives parents permission to do just that: CALM DOWN. Not only is it a joy to read, with wit and humor infused in every chapter, giving us the 'Thank Heaven I am not the only parent who's thought *THAT*!' feeling but it offers tips and tricks to replace bent behaviors we often use in panic and frustration."

—Candace Payne, author, teacher, podcaster

"A delight for any parent who needs a good laugh, *Calm the H*ck Down* rivals the next comedy special in your Netflix queue. Do yourself a favor—skip the show and buy this book instead. I promise you'll laugh just as hard and walk away with some parenting tips that are actually useful. *Calm the H*ck Down* is the permission slip you've been waiting for."

—Ashlee Gadd, founder of *Coffee + Crumbs*

"I don't like parenting books. Am I allowed to say that in an endorsement for a parenting book? But [*Calm the H*ck Down*] is not only hilarious. This book is practical, touching at times, and oh-so-reassuring. If there's anything we need as parents, it's for someone to sidle up alongside us, put their arm around our shoulder, and simply say, 'Yeah, I feel that way, too.' Melanie is the parenting companion we all need."

—Shawn Smucker, author of *The Day the Angels Fell*

CALM the H*CK DOWN

How to Let Go and Lighten Up About Parenting

Melanie Dale

ATRIA PAPERBACK

NEW YORK   LONDON   TORONTO   SYDNEY   NEW DELHI

ATRIA
PAPERBACK

An Imprint of Simon & Schuster, Inc.
1230 Avenue of the Americas
New York, NY 10020

First Atria Paperback edition December 2020

ATRIA PAPERBACK and colophon are trademarks of Simon & Schuster, Inc.

For information about special discounts for bulk
purchases, please contact Simon & Schuster Special Sales at
1-866-506-1949 or business@simonandschuster.com.

The Simon & Schuster Speakers Bureau can bring authors to your live event. For
more information or to book an event, contact the Simon & Schuster Speakers
Bureau at 1-866-248-3049 or visit our website at www.simonspeakers.com.

Interior design by Kyoko Watanabe

Manufactured in the United States of America

1 3 5 7 9 10 8 6 4 2

Library of Congress Control Number: 2020947304

ISBN 978-1-9821-1436-7
ISBN 978-1-9821-1437-4 (ebook)

To Mom and Dad.
This parenting gig is harder than you made it look.

Contents

1. Calm the H*ck Down: 1
Lighten Up About Expectations

2. I'm Sorry for Raising Monsters: 23
Lighten Up About Behavior

3. Talking Is Hard: 47
Lighten Up About Words

4. But What If I Want to Miss Part of My Kid's Childhood?:   61
Lighten Up About Work

5. Can Everyone Please Notice How Awesome I Am?:   79
Lighten Up About Yourself

6. Sleep, Eat, Poop, Repeat: 93
Lighten Up About Bodily Functions

7. Mommy Needs a Time-Out: 119
Lighten Up About Feelings

8. People Are Super Awkward, Including You: 133
Lighten Up About Friends

CONTENTS

9. What Happens in the Backpack Stays in the Backpack: 155
Lighten Up About School

10. Go Team Win the Sportsball!: 171
Lighten Up About Activities

11. Celebrate Good Times, or Don't: 187
Lighten Up About Making Memories

12. When Armpits Awaken: 203
Lighten Up About Big Kids

13. I Hope I Still Like You After They're Gone: 219
Lighten Up About Marriage

14. "Mom, You Only Had Sex the One Time, Right?": 233
Lighten Up About Sex

15. I Worry My Kids Will Be Satanists: 243
Lighten Up About Belief

16. This Too Shall Pass: 259
Lighten Up About the Future

The Lighten Up Guidelines for Laughing at Life 271

Acknowledgments 275

CALM the
H*CK DOWN

Calm the H*ck Down

Lighten Up About Expectations

"Be afraid. Be very afraid."
—The Fly

This is a terrible idea. This book is a broken promise because I told people I wouldn't write a parenting book. I promised profusely it would never happen. We are a mess over here. I like to win awards and achieve stuff so I think I can safely say that I am The Number One Worst Mom ever to write a parenting book. Somebody, give me a trophy. Aren't you excited? You will feel so good about yourself when you're done with this thing.

I hate parenting books. It's not their fault. It's me. Every time I see a parenting book, I think it doesn't apply to me because they don't know my kids or the disturbing cesspool of my shriveled heart. I am the worst, and that shiny book could not possibly understand how truly hideous I am at this job, which seems to come so effortlessly to even the basest of human beings. Stop judging me, Book, with your easy-to-apply tips and promises that

I'll never yell again and that my children will rise up and call me blessed. No, they won't. I just asked them.

I feel threatened by most parenting books, not because they aren't written by fabulous parents but because I feel like they're only applicable to rainbow-pooping unicorns who have zero issues. That's probably not true, but I dedicate plenty of side-eye for most parenting websites and books that want to help me with my problems. I can't tell you about the specific things my kids are dealing with because that's their business, but in case your first response to my call to "lighten up" is to think, "If you only knew my life and what my kids were like . . ." or "That author can suck it," let me assure you that you're in good company. In addition to all the typical stuff that comes with raising humans, we have quite a bit going on in the doctors, therapists, and labels department around here. I spend a large amount of my parenting time at school meetings, therapy, doctor appointments, and waiting in line at the pharmacy, and sometimes venturing out into the world can feel almost unbearable.

The other day my husband, Alex, was like, "How can you write a book about calming down and lightening up? Look at us! Do we seem calm?"

And I shot back, "Are you kidding me? It's because I'm practicing what I preach that I'm still here, that I can get up and face these shenanigans every day and keep going. If I wasn't learning how to lighten up about every aspect of parenting, I would've left a long time ago. We are where we are precisely because I'm learning to let go of what doesn't matter and calm the heck down."

So, if you have some hard stuff going on in your home, solidarity. We do, too, and I don't just mean my kid got a B+. Because they can tell their own stories someday and don't need me airing the nitty gritty of their lives, this book isn't an exposé about all my kids' stuff. It's about me parenting them. If your kid doesn't fit the mold, if your kid is atypical, or mentally ill, or physically ill, if the needs are obvious for all to see or hidden beneath the surface, you're welcome here.

I am tapping this out on my phone while sitting at tumbling practice because somewhere along the way I became a cheer mom. I'm also an adoptive mom, an in vitro mom, a swim mom, soccer mom, lacrosse mom, mom of a teenager, mom of some tweenagers, special needs mom, and probably a deranged mom.

I have three kids. People like to compare parenting to basketball. If you grow from two kids to three, they say, "You've gone from man-to-man to zone." I love March Madness as much as any girl from Kentucky, but this metaphor doesn't quite work, because even if you do have a partner, how often are you both on the court at the same time? I liken parenting more to juggling. You start with a ball, or two if it's twinsies, and you toss it up and down for a while until it feels doable. Then maybe you add a ball. Then another. With each ball you add, it gets more complicated, but you eventually adjust. You add a new variable, a flaming baton or maybe a chainsaw, then you adjust to that, too. If you have a partner, when you're together, you develop a funky routine tossing the balls back and forth. If you have enough balls, you might draw a crowd. Wow, you guys are really good at this. Like, Harlem Globetrotters good. And at the point you get cocky, someone points a tennis ball machine at your face and pummels you with balls until you're in the fetal position on the ground begging for mercy.

My kids come from three different continents, out of birth order. Elliott was a preemie my body tried to kill in utero. Evie was adopted from Ethiopia as a toddler, Ana from Latvia as a nine-year-old, and they had lives and families before ours. My kids are awesome. Obviously, I'm proud. Of them. I, on the other hand, do not know what I'm doing. We are making it up as we go. I see a therapist because my kids' therapist told me to and I'm very obedient, unlike my kids, who are . . . what are we supposed to call them now? Leaders. They have super-good leadership skills, aka they are belligerent a-holes. (If you're reading this, kids, I assume you'll take that as a compliment.)

I can trace my journey of calming the heck down to five moments. If I was a superhero in the Marvel Cinematic Universe, these moments would make it into the montage at the beginning of my origin story, for sure.

Moment One: My stress affected my child. When I was pregnant with Elliott, after years of infertility, I wanted to make everything perfect for him. I would make all the perfect choices and research how to be the best mom ever. About halfway through, other judgy parents and too much reading freaked me out. I thought for sure I'd already screwed up my baby, and I hadn't even met him yet, and I started sobbing uncontrollably until suddenly I felt my uterus contract. I realized that my stress level affected my physical body, and the body of the child inside me.

Moment Two: I couldn't control what happened to my child. A couple years into our adoption process with Evie, we got some hard news and thought we might never be able to bring her home. I sat at a red light in my minivan and felt the full weight of the lack of control roll over me like a wave.

Moment Three: I didn't know how much time we had together. The first time we met Ana, she visited us for a summer, and we fell utterly in love with her. She built forts with Evie and Elliott, her bubbly laugh filled the house, and every day was an adventure. After cuddling together and reading hours of bed-time stories, throwing her a birthday party, and developing that comfortable feeling like she'd always been here, one morning I had to put her on a plane, not knowing if I'd ever see her again. Two governments and a whole lot of people had to agree to let her come back, and we had no way of knowing how it would all turn out.

Moment Four: Parenting looked different than I'd planned. After twelve years of assembling our kids, I thought we were done with the hard part, but then we went through a season I call "Labelpalooza," when I kept finding myself in rooms with experts telling me various diagnoses about some of my people. Sitting in an office across from a neuropsychologist while she shared her testing results with us, everything felt surreal.

Moment Five: Somewhere along the way, I'd learned to parent. Sipping coffee at a table full of young moms before I got up to speak at their event, they asked me questions, and I shared some of the ways I've handled things with the kids. One of the moms said, "Oh, my gosh, you're so wise. I'm writing this down." I looked at her, surprised, and thought, *Wait, do I, like, know stuff now?*

I thought that was hilarious, but as I've spent time with moms around the country and sipped coffee with them before they graciously allowed me to speak at their events, I've discovered that they're all freaking out about parenting. And at this point, I've figured out how to calm down about a lot of it, not because I'm amazing, but because I've had to. Rocky pregnancy? Check. Scary doctor appointments? Check check. Occupational therapy? Trauma therapy? Speech therapy? Play therapy? Attachment therapy? Fill-in-the-blank therapy? English as a second language? Transracial parenting? Toddler adoption? Older child adoption? Adopting out of birth order? Special services at school? Checkity check check. I obviously don't know anybody's unique situation, but my parenting education on the fly has been broad and fairly thorough.

I realized through these conversations with other parents in different parts of the country that we all have something in common. We're all freaking out and wondering if we're doing it right. And the best and most important thing we can do for our kids is to calm the heck down.

All the challenges we've faced as a family gave me the beautiful gift of smashing any expectations I had going into this thing. From the get-go, as they jammed the needle into my spine before cutting me open to rescue my son six weeks early, I learned that parenting wasn't going to turn out the way I thought. My kids keep reminding me, again and again, that they are not here to perform for me. Which pisses me off because when you look up "people pleaser" on the Googleweb, there's a picture of me doing jazz hands asking how high you want me to jump. People pleasing got me into plenty of trouble, though, so maybe it's better I'm raising fighters. They'll make incredible adults if they can survive their childhoods.

After assembling our family for twelve years of scary hard work with doctors, lawyers, needles, and paperwork, sometimes my husband and I wonder out loud if there's a way to undo it, like a reset button. What were we thinking? We're really bad at this. Surely these wonderful kids could find better adults to raise them. Usually that's when a caring friend says something about God giving us exactly the kids we're supposed to have and we're the right people for the job and God doesn't call the qualified, God qualifies the called, but I usually zone out and think about zombies or spaceships or a spaceship filled with zombies. Ooh!

Screenplay idea. Somebody write the crap out of that show because I will binge it like a bag of Doritos.

I'm concerned that the people in my real life who know me will question why I would ever try to write a parenting book. One time I spoke at a local moms' group, and then a few weeks later I ran into one of the moms at the grocery store and she said, "Oh! That's a lot of alcohol in your cart!" I blamed it on my husband. (Sorry, Alex.) I accidentally taught my oldest a new swear word yesterday. I never wear a bra to the bus stop. Parenting is not how I thought it would be.

The greatest achievement I've got going for me is that I stay. I show up every day and laugh in the face of this difficult job with no benefits or vacation days. I assume we will survive. Sometimes I call my husband on the way home from therapy and threaten to keep driving and never come back, but I come home again and again, because these people need their meds, and I'm the only one who knows where we keep the toilet paper. And shuts drawers. I'm the only drawer shutter in the whole house. I don't understand this. If I wasn't here, all the drawers and cabinets would stay wide open with their contents spilling out for all the world to see. So, I have job security. These little buggers need me to shut their drawers.

I also don't know how to write a parenting book without swearing. I'll do my best.

We need to lighten up about parenting. We take it way too seriously. Listen, I know these are people's lives we're playing with, but let's all dial it down a notch or two. I mean, we made it through our childhoods relatively intact. I'm in therapy, can't reproduce, and am admitting in a parenting book that I don't know how to parent, but other than those small things, I'm completely fine. I'm not the only one, though, right? None of us really knows what we're doing, and the second we think we do, our kids change like that spinning cornucopia in the seventy-fifth Hunger Games. Tick tock.

The first parenting magazine I ever read freaked me out about the danger of invisible bat bites giving our babies rabies, and the other day I listened to a mom go on for forty-five minutes about whether or not she should call her kid's counselor . . . in college. From birth to empty nesting, we read too much, plan too much, engineer too much, and probably give ourselves things like ulcers and diarrhea.

We run ourselves ragged trying to be and do and give everything our kids need, and the only way to keep up this pace is if we start giving new parents Time-Turners like Hermione Granger's in *Harry Potter and the Prisoner of Azkaban*. "Congrats, Mom and Dad, on your new baby. Here's your birth certificate and your Time-Turner to help you be two places at once for the foreseeable future. Good luck!" In the *New York Times* article "The Relentlessness of Modern Parenting," Claire Cain Miller writes,

> The time parents spend in the presence of their children has not changed much, but parents today spend more of it doing hands-on child care. Time spent on activities like reading to children; doing crafts; taking them to lessons; attending recitals and games; and helping with homework has increased the most. Today, mothers spend nearly five hours a week on that, compared with 1 hour 45 minutes in 1975—and they worry it's not enough.[1]

---

1 Claire Cain Miller, "The Relentlessness of Modern Parenting," *New York Times*, December 25, 2018. https://www.nytimes.com/2018/12/25/upshot/the-relentlessness -of-modern-parenting.html.

We are out of control. And I could've been the worst. I'm a type A control freak who wants to raise perfect automatons to people please the heck out of everyone around them. Instead, I ended up with strong-willed kids who do what they want when they want. I've had to learn to let go and laugh or else they will turn on me and shove my head on a pike like in *Lord of the Flies*. Instead of guiding them as an orderly, nineteenth-century schoolmarm like I pictured, I'm more like a pinball machine, flicking them chaotically toward the direction I want them to head except for when they blast right by me and end up in the hole. I've adapted.

If you feel like parenting is devouring you, if your pressures and expectations are making you dread every day, then this book will help you lighten up. Maybe go to the doc and get some meds, too. But bring this book while you're getting them. By the end, you'll feel one of two things: *I feel like I can lighten up about raising these kids*, or *At least I'm a better parent than she is*. I call either of those scenarios a win.

I Thought I'd Be Amazing at Parenting, So Color Me Surprised

Did anybody else think they'd be better at this? I thought we'd be better than we actually are. It seemed like we'd nail this thing when we were merely armchair parents observing others at the grocery store and restaurants. Other people's kids would totally wig out in the produce aisle and I'd think to myself, *See? When I'm a parent I'm going to include my young child in the decision-making process for dinner. I'll let him choose what veggie he wants, and we'll go home and cook it together.* Once I became a parent, that happened one time. Every other time, I'd wheel my cart directly to the bakery for the free cookie, buying myself five minutes of cookie gnawing to race around the store throwing food in my cart like that lady on the shopping sweepstakes before my kid would wiggle out of the seat belt and start grabbing things from the shelves.

We were going to be awesome, until we had kids. And now that we have them, we compare ourselves to other parents, we compare our kids to other kids, and we have this sneaking suspicion that everyone is pulling it off except us, and everyone else's kids are Mensa-level smart and never eat woodchips or duct tape their siblings to the kitchen table. When we realize we're not measuring up to our pre-parent ideals, we panic and take to the internet and parenting books, where we truly discover what losers we are. It's worse than we thought. We freak out, and the only thing that seems to help is freaking out with other parents.

Or maybe you're not worried. Yet. If you're the only one not panicking, then you think there's something wrong with you. Why are you so calm? Don't you love your kids? You dig deep and start freaking out to fit in and prove that you, too, love your children. Your kids were fine eating regular butter from the dairy aisle, but someone told you butter causes instant sterilization, and now, after spending all afternoon researching butters and talking to other parents who are freaking out about butter, you drive an hour out of town to a farm, where you invest in grass-fed butter from locally milked, non-GMO cows receiving cow yoga and udder massage. Now you feel uppity about your butter, warn other people about butter danger, and we all buy more books, read more articles, and the panic grows.

The thing is, we don't notice how nuts we are until it's too late, because we're like that lobster getting boiled alive. Or is it a frog? I don't know fancy food. We start off in cool water, enjoying a nice swim with our new spawn, and then the water starts to heat up around us incrementally. We think, *Hey, somebody sent me an article about what helps brain development in utero and my doctor gave me these prenatal vitamins. A few minor changes because I love my kid. Awesome. I'm amazing. Look how selfless I'm being. I haven't had wine in three months. Somebody, give me Parent of the Year.*

When you're popping those prenatal pills, then crushing organic veggies into homemade baby food, you're doing all this to develop your baby's brain. You think you want a big-brained superbaby, but as your kid starts growing up, eating Play-Doh, and biting other kids at day care, you start to lower your expectations. Huh. Maybe if I sign him up for some music classes, that'll fix it. You find yourself sitting in a circle with other parents each week while the kids shake maracas, but your kid just wants to beat himself in the head with the maracas. Then he bites one of the other kids. The horror. Why is your child so violent? You microwaved your lunch meat for nine months and avoided sushi. Is this because you had a C-section? Does he have a proclivity for violence and knives because that's the first thing he saw in the world? You start picturing jail time. Your baby does look good in orange. You imagine a lifetime of conversations on phones looking through that Plexiglass partition thingy. Your baby loves his plastic phone he got for Christmas. You lower your expectations a tad more. Maybe instead of a superbaby you could be content with a non–serial killer. Instead of Neil deGrasse Tyson, you aim for not Jeffrey Dahmer.

I never thought I'd doubt myself so much. I never thought I'd blame myself so much for every little foible and failing. I promised I'd never yell. I totally yell. I told myself I'd be patient. Should've known parenting didn't come with a personality transplant. And here's the kicker. I thought I'd enjoy parenting more. I don't.

Don't get me wrong, I love my kids and really enjoy a tremendous amount of the parenting action I see. But there are some parts that just aren't enjoyable. It's not all fun and games. Well, there are a lot of games, but they cease to be fun when it's your eighth round of Candy Land or you're sitting in a rainy stadium watching your cheerleader spell B-E-A-G-G-R-E-S-S-I-V-E five hundred times.

I've disappointed myself with how underwhelming I am as a parent. Other parents seem to have it together better. They always remember their kids' school account logins, they pack awesome lunches, and they enjoy every second of a poetry recitation contest, even other people's kid's poems, even the sixth child in a row doing Shel Silverstein. Or maybe the other parents are better at faking it. Maybe none of us are getting it all right, but we can't tell because no one can see past their own shortcomings. Maybe there's no such thing as straight A's in parenting. Perish the thought.

Before you can lighten up about the expectations you had for parenting, first you have to mourn those expectations. Did you think it would come easy to you? Did you think your kids would be more like you or less like you? Maybe you played basketball so you hoped your kid would play basketball. Maybe your child is facing an unexpected diagnosis. Maybe you told yourself you'd never yell at your kids.

Make a list, write an essay, or, if you hate writing, then stare at a wall and think hard about the expectations you had going into parenting. Write or say all your expectations out loud, and then let yourself mourn the fact that life didn't turn out that way. This doesn't take anything away from your real kids. Mourning your imaginary unicorn kids in your brain frees you up to love the unique, incredible kids you actually have. Mourning your delusions of parental grandeur frees you up to accept yourself as the loving loser you actually are. Take a moment to be honest with yourself. Are you comparing your kids to the fake ones in your dreams? Are you comparing yourself with an airbrushed, glossy pinup version of a parent? Are you comparing yourself with the neighbor down the street?

Whether other parents are faking it or actually amazeballs, I have a tried and true method for overcoming my comparison issues. When you see other parents who seem to have it all together, picture their bathrooms at home and make them gross. You don't know what their real bathrooms look like, but when you meet SuperMom at soccer practice, the best way to survive that with your dignity intact is to visualize her bathroom at home. Her boys have peed up the walls, and there's something greenish growing in the corner. Her daughter likes to smear an entire tube of toothpaste all over the sink each night, and SuperMom has been too busy being awesome on the outside to deal with any of this. When she's handing out her perfect snacks dressed in her bangin' Lululemon yoga outfit that showcases her perfectly sculpted butt, think about her awful, gag-worthy bathroom and feel a sense of camaraderie. Because even if we can pull off a decent look out in the world, we all have that bathroom waiting for us back home.

What a Preemie and an English Language Learner Taught Me

"My boy, Silas, started walking at eight months! He was doing long division by four years old, and he's already on his fifth language! But I can't take any credit for it. He's a natural because of how I read to him for five hours every day when he was a baby."

"Coraline, my nine-year-old, just got pre-pre-pre-accepted into Harvard and we're really hashtag blessed."

Part of what makes us feel like sucky parents is listening to everyone else humblebrag about their kids' accomplishments. Post your kid's report card on Facebook one more time, *Karen*.

(I just took a break from writing to check on the kids and found that one of them had painted a box bright red then chucked all the brushes, covered in wet red paint, into our antique family heirloom cabinet. As you can imagine, I handled this with grace, poise, and a touch of whimsy, celebrating her artistic endeavor and bold attempt to skip steps in the cleanup process. Just kidding, I yelled. I yelled so hard. Now, where was I on unpacking my expert parenting advice?)

My body wasn't keen on being pregnant. It tried to tell me through the years of infertility, but I finally banged it into submission. By week thirty-four, the preeclampsia, partially abrupted placenta, and intrauterine growth restriction were finally too much to take, so in a lovely effort to keep me from stroking out, the good doctors cut Elliott out of me and whisked him up to the NICU to recover in an incubator spa. He even had tiny goggles over his eyes to protect them from the bilirubin lights. He looked like he was in a baby tanning bed, and I worried about sunscreen. He comes from moley stock.

You know those checklists they go through at the pediatrician's at each checkup appointment? "Does he have over fifty words?" "Is he walking?" and "Is he doing advanced calculus yet?" Weighing in at four pounds and already a prizefighter for surviving my toxic womb, Elliott was behind on every single thing on the chart.

For the first few years of his life, we didn't have a lot of check marks. My kiddo wasn't fully baked, so he took awhile to catch up. And I'm glad. Having a preemie was the best thing that could've happened to break me out of competitive parenting. When people bragged to me about their walking, talking wonders, I smiled. *Wow. That's so great for you.* My kid developed in his own time, and I learned to love him for it. These days he's both bigger and smarter than me, so it all worked out.

A few years later, when Ana came to live with us, I was instantly hurled into tween parenting. I sat in school meetings listening to the other parents ask questions about grades and test scores, and I knew nothing. Up till then, I'd been hanging out in the land of sight words and preschool craft projects with Elliott and Evie, and now here I was learning about these statewide tests that all the big kids had to pass. Stress! Goals! Something called a Lexile level! While the other kids at school were acing tests and probably reading *War and Peace*, Ana was learning her third language and second alphabet. She flunked her eye exam, and everyone thought she couldn't see, when really, she didn't know the English alphabet. Having an English language learner and marveling as my daughter figured out a whole new life on the fly taught me so much. I learned that there is no one way to quantify success. Ana not only learned English but learned a whole teen vernacular that's beyond me. These days I'm the one catching up.

Me: You're so lit, honey! And I mean the cool lit not the drunk one! And also not *literature*. Lit. That's what the kids are saying these days, right?

Ana: Oh my gosh, please stop.

15

Me: You're the GOAT. That's Greatest of All Time. You're totes that.

Ana: Wow.

Your kids will change how you see the world. They'll shatter your expectations in more ways than you can imagine. Throughout our kids' lives, there are so many trophies and awards. We have expectations for our kids, and they inevitably do things their own way, whether by choice or by necessity. We watch our sweaty little miracles work so hard at the things unseen by the rest of the world. Your babies have achievements that only you know about. I wish there were trophies for the invisible achievements. I wish there were trophies for our invisible achievements, too. We are doing so much right, but sometimes we focus on all the ways we miss the mark.

I award you, dear parent, the Didn't Yell Today Cup (I didn't earn that one today; thanks, red paint). You get the Made Dinner on Two Hours of Sleep Certificate. Here's the At the Hospital with a Sick Child and Still Have to Go to Work Trophy. We may feel like losers most of the time, but we're pretty flipping fantastic.

Also, it's okay to suck at some stuff. Maybe you are a total loser in one or two areas, and that's okay. We don't all have to be good at everything. There's this expectation that we're supposed to meet all our kids' needs, but that's impossible. They need way too much. I cannot be three places at once, and I certainly can't coach soccer. Instead of approaching parenting like a sole proprietor business, we need to approach it like a large company, with divisions for everything. One parent is the sportsball coach. One's bringing killer snacks. One works at the DMV and makes sure we all can still drive our minivans. Somebody volunteer to hold babies at church, somebody be a doctor and cure their ear infections, and somebody else chaperone the school field trip. We all have several jobs to do, but we don't have to do them all.

Think through your routines. Are you trying to be awesome at everything? Is there something you need to calm the heck down about? Are you freaking out about butter? Maybe it's not butter, but whatever "butter" is for you, think through if you can cut out some steps. Are you going to more than two grocery stores a week on the hunt for magic ingredients? How many times a month are you logging in to your son's school account to check his grades? There are some areas in our lives that we can't simplify, but can you simplify a noncritical area to lighten your load? For instance, we have a team around some of us dealing with medicines and therapies, and those things are here to stay right now. I can't do anything about those things. But what I can do is break up with baking and say no to crafts. Other people can do those. I can suck at those and excel in something else.

Lower your expectations for your kids to be superhuman in all categories. And lower the expectations on yourself. Stop killing yourself competing with other parents and let the milestones, awards, and benchmarks fall away. So, we thought we'd be better at this than we are. We thought parenting would be a slam dunk. Whatever. We don't need that kind of pressure in our lives.

Good Enough Expectations

We tend to have two modes when it comes to expectations for stuff. Mode One is blind excitement. *This experience is going to blow my kids' minds. They are going to get along perfectly. Everyone is going to be healthy. They are going to be overcome with gratitude for how much I love them. I am amazing.* Mode Two is doomsday thinking. *This experience is going to be a clustercluck. My kids are going to fight the whole time, decide they hate me, and sacrifice me to appease a volcano god. Someone will most likely die horribly.* It's my experience that most things fall somewhere in between, we all survive, and our kids will even have a few decent memories from their childhoods. I've learned to swap my great expectations for good enough expectations.

Depending on how you're wired, you may need to lower your expectations or possibly raise them. Some of us assume everything will be awesome, and some assume everything will crash and burn. So, I'll say tweak your expectations. Ask yourself, "Am I expecting too much from this person or situation?" "Am I expecting too little?" Calm down and aim for good enough. With most situations in parenting, it's a mixed bag and you'll probably come out with a few lessons, a few fun memories, some laughs, and one or two moments you'd like to expunge permanently from your brain.

To combat impossible standards and the pressure of crazy expectations, you may need to narrow your world. If you have too many conflicting voices in your head, too many people up in your business, whittle down your insiders. You might need to limit social media, stop hanging out with the people who are stressing you out, and read less. (I mean clickbait internet articles and other people's Facebook feeds. Keep reading this very important book, 'kay? Thanks.) I mean, read more, read lots more, but put up some healthy blinders when it comes to posts and articles about every possible thing we're supposed to be enraged and freaked out about. This amount of input is not sustainable for human life.

When I was pregnant, I learned that I needed to narrow my world, because the amount of information out there was destroying me and, subsequently, the poor boy trapped inside me. We have access to so much info, from people, print, and podcasts, and I decided to give myself less access. I didn't need to know about every possible thing that could go wrong. No human should have to carry the burden of literally everything. I narrowed my focus, made my world a little smaller, and decided to calm down and enjoy this baby no matter what. This decision came in handy as my pregnancy tanked and my birth plan became an adorable fairy tale.

Or maybe instead of narrowing your world, you need to broaden yours. Maybe you're feeling the pressure of expectations because you're surrounded by friends or family who do everything the same and you're expected to conform. Broaden your mind. Get out and discover other ways of doing things and recognize the value in other people's choices. We don't all have to be the same.

I have a regular practice I call "Palms-Up Parenting" that I employ when I feel the pressure of perfectionism and the worries that I'll somehow mess up my kids starting to make me frizzy. Take a deep breath and ball up your fists. Now release your breath and fists and hold out your hands palms up. I say a three-word prayer with this: "God, they're yours." Or you can just breathe. Palms-Up Parenting reminds me to parent with an open hand instead of a closed fist. I can't control every aspect of their lives with an iron grip. I have to loosen up. I practice this whenever I want to go Full Gollum, snatch up my kids, clench my fists, and hiss, "My precioussss." Last week I had to practice Palms-Up Parenting when I had the brilliant idea to read *Pet Sematary* while vacationing at a beach house on a busy highway.

Expectations—the ones people have for us, the ones we put on our kids, and the ones we have for ourselves—can leave us frustrated and frazzled. We're expected to be perfect parents who raise perfect kids, and that's exhausting, not to mention impossible. Thankfully, there's another way. We need to calm the h*ck down.

10 WAYS TO STAY CALM-ISH

1. Laugh at yourself regularly. Cultivate a healthy sense of humor.
2. Put yourself in time-out for a few minutes. Go sit on the stairs, hide in the bathroom, or take a quick bubble bath.
3. Take a walk and get some fresh air.
4. Make a top ten list of all the things you did well today. Read it out loud in the mirror.
5. Swear into a pillow. (My friend Jenni flips her kids the bird under the table. Don't judge until you have teenagers.)
6. Sing karaoke in the kitchen or at your desk if you have your own office. (Might be awkward in a shared space, but you do you.) You can find great online karaoke on the Karaoke Channel on YouTube or karafun.com.
7. Say something you're grateful for. Gratitude trumps crappy 'tude.
8. Do a forward fold. Plant your feet hip-width apart, bend at the waist, and let your arms dangle toward the ground.

Nod your head yes. Feel the stretch in the back of your legs.
Be careful as you stand up, so you don't pass out.

9. Have coffee or something stronger with a friend. Good
friends can diffuse our stress and help us feel like we're not
alone.

10. Hug your kid.

2

I'm Sorry for Raising Monsters

Lighten Up About Behavior

"Would your family welcome a serious
investigation of these disturbances by someone
who can make firsthand observations?"
—Poltergeist

I probably should go easy on my kids, because at least they aren't criminals, unlike their parents. One time, Alex and I accidentally helped a kid steal someone's golf cart.

I'm not sure if this makes it better or worse, but we didn't realize we were abetting a crime until later. We thought we were helping a neighbor in distress. So, either we're hardened criminals or just super stupid.

First, I should explain about the golf carts. Prepare yourself, because I'm about to sound so suburban you might break out into chinos and inexplicably find yourself edging a patch of unruly grass. I live in a community in Georgia where we all drive around in golf carts. There are miles and miles of golf cart paths

23

through neighborhoods and wetlands, and we putter around on these little electric wonders to the grocery store, school, the library, and even our outdoor amphitheater to hear Journey and Bon Jovi cover bands and watch our drunk neighbors. I like to joke that between my electric golf cart and my minivan, I drive a hybrid.

When we first moved down to Georgia, Elliott was a mere baby, and I didn't yet spend most of my time carpooling to one million hours of swim team practices. So, Alex and I were out for a leisurely stroll in our new golf cart one night when we came upon a young lad pushing his own golf cart in the woods in the dark. We approached the teen and offered to help him get home safely, and he very politely waved us off. We would hear none of it and got out to help push. I say we, but I mean Alex, who is much more helpful than I am. I am perfectly content to leave a young man-child on the side of the road in the dark, assuming he has a plan. One time we took personality tests to discover our strengths and I scored a zero in the "mercy" category. Fend for yourselves, because Melanie is not here for you.

Thankfully, I've partnered myself with a very generous, giving man who will definitely stop and help you on the side of the road. Which is why I blame him entirely for this thievery.

"Oh no! Did you lose your shoe?" we exclaimed, seeing the teen was limping along wearing only one shoe. He nodded in the affirmative and kept pushing the golf cart.

"Is the cart out of battery?" This is a common occurrence in our land of electric golf carts that lose their charges regularly. The city has installed plug-in stations around the community, but you haven't lived here till you've stranded yourself somewhere at least once.

"I lost the key," he explained. Why we didn't see "no key" as a red flag is beyond me. Alex and the boy pushed the cart into his neighborhood, he thanked us, and we took off. A hundred yards down the path, we discovered his missing shoe, so we turned around, found the boy in his neighborhood, and delivered his shoe. He thanked us again and tried to get away. We assumed he was overcome with gratitude to the two strangers helping him. We were new to the genteel Deep South and thought we were knocking it out of the park with our charming neighborliness. I was already starting to work in some "y'alls," and now we'd been friendly. We were so amazing.

As we drove away feeling great about ourselves, we started to talk through the situation. Why would you let your shoe fall off and not run back and grab it? How could you lose your golf cart key? Why did he not want us to help him and keep trying to hurry up and get away from us?

"Honey, I think we just helped that boy steal somebody's golf cart."

The South is so lucky to have us. As are our children, who have nothing to worry about, since their parents' behavior is worse than anything they can concoct on their own. Parents freak out about their kids' behavior all the time, and it helps to remember what we were like, or are currently like, and calm down. I have a sneaking suspicion our kids are smarter than we were.

I Worry I'm Raising Monsters

I'm probably raising monsters and it's a good thing they're cute. Our family doesn't do subtle or demure, so we stomp through life leaving very large maniacal footprints. My kids came to get down. They speak up, blurt out, make messes, and leave a swath of debris in their wake. From what archeologists will find during a dig on our property thousands of years from now, our kind subsisted on Sharpies and glitter.

My husband mentioned that it might be nice to assure you that I actually like our kids. Apparently, I can sound a bit negative about parenting, which is so weird after the morning I had cleaning up the bathroom. (Look for my next book in this series, *Why Is There Pee Everywhere All the Time?*)

But yes, parenting is great. Everyone should totally try it. For a few hours. By babysitting someone's puppy.

No, seriously, have you ever been caught off guard by how awesome your kids are? I mean, maybe it's not surprising to you, but I get so excited when I catch my kids being amazing behind my back.

One time, Evie's teacher came up to me in church, smiled, and said, "I just love having Evie in my class! She's so great." Since we were in church, I don't even think she was lying. When people say nice things about my kids, I can't be cool about it. I blurted out, "Really?!" I need to start practicing receiving compliments in front of a mirror. *Thank you. I know. Isn't she, though?* It's amazing to discover when our hard work at home pays off out in the wide world. Makes me think someday our kids will have jobs and pay rent so they can move out.

Positivity!

A few weeks ago, we checked Ana's phone, because parenting a teen means going full *Harriet the Spy* on her when she least expects it. And what did we find? Texts letting her friends know about our rules. She didn't even mention that she thinks the rules are asinine. And when we did a deep dive into her email, we found a thank-you note to an authority figure. Good grief, are our children . . . polite and kind? How did we not know this? I felt parental pride swell up in my bosomly area, and Ana wanted to know how much longer I'd be crying about how proud I was into her hair. "Just a few more minutes," I gasped.

I worry my kids will be monsters, but over and over they reveal how incredible they are. Somehow, they've risen above my crippling sarcasm to become lovely human beings. The older they get, the more I like them. That's been my favorite thing about parenting: discovering that not only do I love my children, but I like them as well. They can be extremely likable, especially if I've had enough coffee.

And as for the areas that are . . . less than enjoyable . . . I'm pretty sure it's my fault.

My kids love to argue, and I wonder why and then I realize . . . oh. Apple, meet Tree. We're five thriving arguers who all think they're 100 percent right at all times. I spent three days last week locked in an all-out battle with my teen about whether or not Persephone is a biblical character. She was absolutely convinced that Persephone, the wife of Hades, one of the big three in Greek mythology, shows up in the Bible somewhere and I could not convince her otherwise. She spent days poring through the Bible, a rather weighty book, looking for Persephone. Argumentative scripture reading is so on point with our family values of Dying on a Hill and Being Emphatic. But, hey, she was reading a Bible, so look at me challenging her in her spiritual formation. Of course, using a religious text to win an argument has never hurt anyone ever. No danger there (hashtag sarcasm font). Also, it was the graphic novel version of the Bible, so she was probably just hunting for any illustration of a chick wearing a chiton with a laurel wreath in her hair.

Our kids think they're so logical all the time. I know I did when I was their age. My parents called me Little Miss Lawyer because I had an argument for everything and wouldn't stop until I won. Now that I have a teen daughter, I know I wasn't beating them with my superior intellectual prowess. They were just walking away before they lost control and stapled my mouth shut. Actually, in junior high when I asked if I could get another piercing, my dad joked the only other piercing I could get was to pierce my lips together. Touché. Now I make words for a living, so who's laughing now, Daddy?

If only kids would show up in this life as perfectly logical adults, but with that new-baby smell. The truth is, you're going to spend a couple decades of your life disciplining them into fully formed adults. These things don't just happen. Sometimes I expect my kids to think logically, but they lack the development and experience needed to navigate situations. They are going to screw up a lot, either by carelessness or wanton disregard for the rules. It's okay, and you'll get through. They won't be axe murderers (probably).

There are two types of parents in the world. People who assume their kids could never do anything wrong and people who assume their kids totally did it. My mom was the latter. She didn't want to be caught with her parental pants down, the naïve mom shaking her head going, "My child would never do that," while all the other parents were snickering that they saw her child do exactly that and with a crap ton of people. We've all met that parent.

"I taught my darling Ursula to solve things with words and not fists." Uh-huh. Is that your darling whaling on my kid in the

Chick-fil-A playland over there, because I see hair-pulling and I think she just screamed, "Hold my sippy cup!" These days if our kids get into trouble, there's probably proof on Instagram somewhere just waiting for their first employer to find.

Most kids operate somewhere in between Mother Teresa and Charles Manson. There's a lot of wiggle room in there, although I do think all three-year-olds are raging sociopaths. So, let's assume our kids are definitely messing up but they're probably not irredeemable at this point. A little guidance should clean up the rough edges and turn them into socially responsible citizens somewhere down the line. Maybe.

Bribery and Boomerangs

When it comes to discipline, I try to focus on one quantifiable thing at a time. For instance, with one of my healthy arguers, I focus on "Obey the first time." I say this a lot. Since we all love the arguing so very much, it's easy to get locked into a debate about every little thing, and debating everything from bath time to a peanut butter sandwich all day long wears me down to a nub. *I commend you for your tenacity. But do the frick what I say.* Someday our kids' independence will be an asset, but they still have to learn how to take direction from the authorities in their lives. Better to learn that from us than from the prison warden.

Focusing on one thing at a time, especially when the kids are younger, helps them work on the thing that really matters. I had to learn to lighten up and let the unimportant stuff slide. Does it matter if their socks match? Not really, no. My husband and I are both wordy people, so we've had to practice using fewer words.

Resist the urge to lecture. Keep the explanation simple. We boil down the lectures to tapes we can repeat. "Obey the first time." "If you mess it up, clean it up." "Press pause." That last one is great for when they're getting into their feelings, but we have to do things like find shoes and get out the door. *The feelings are important, but we need to press pause on them, get our butts in the car, and then you can continue emoting.* My kids all understand the pause button on video games and TV, so this usually works.

As often as possible, I allow natural consequences to play out. She throws her toy and now she doesn't have her toy anymore. He didn't wear a coat and now he's cold. (Obviously I'm not talking about subzero arctic weather here. I'm talking small consequences, not losing a foot.) He refused to do his chores and now he can't play. Have them write an apology letter to the person they hurt. If your kid misses the bus, make her pay for a Mommy Uber ride.

If they've hurt their brother or sister, I make them serve that person. Do their chores, bring them dinner, carry their laundry. If they break something, they earn the money to pay for it. When one of my kids stole something from another, we made Kid A do chores to earn money for a small safe for Kid B. "You'll pay for her to have peace of mind with her belongings since you took that away from her." Kid B was super stoked about having a fancy safe like in a hotel and Kid A learned that crime doesn't pay. Speaking of chores, I'm almost happy when my kids step out of line because we get a ton of stuff done around here.

We use both positive and negative reinforcement, depending on the situation. I do a whole lot of positive reinforcement, aka "bribery." What do they want? Find the carrot you can dangle and dangle it hard, letting them earn things like gum, an app, ice cream money, lip balm, iTunes card, or screen time. And then sometimes when positive reinforcement isn't working, a little negative reinforcement will. What do they want? Take it away from them. Tighten up the reins and take away a privilege, like a toy, time with friends, screen time, or their phone.

As your kids get older, treat them like boomerangs. They ask to go somewhere, you say yes, and you release them out and then watch them come back. Out and back, out and back. Every time they come back right on time, that builds trust. If the boomerang doesn't come back on time, or the boomerang takes a side trip, tighten up a bit and bring them closer to home for a while.

We teach our kids that lying is the worst. If they mess up, the best thing they can do is come clean, and we can figure it out together. Lying puts a chink in the relationship, and then it takes time to rebuild trust. I'm always happy when my kids choose honesty, and I generally lessen their sentence when they plead guilty. One of my kids ate the other's candy. If they'd been honest, I would've made them buy their sibling new candy and write an apology note. But since they lied about it, and we found the wrappers in their trash can, they got a couple weeks restricted from screen time, too.

Sometimes things happen around here, and no one admits it was them, and I start to wonder if there's a ghost in the house messing with our stuff. Those situations can be tricky when you can't pin it on anyone, so you don't know who to hold responsible. I've gotten to where I don't care about a confession. Confessions are great, but if it's not happening and you can't eat anyone's brain to discover the truth, like Liv Moore on *iZombie*, then say, "I believe you. You didn't do it. But as a family we all pitch in when things get messy, so I'm giving you this job." When kids refuse to admit who perpetrated the crime, treat it like a jump ball and take turns with who has to deal with it. "No One clogged this toilet? Okay, well it's your turn to clean up No One's poop." I'm sure the Faceless Men had to deal with this all the time in the House of Black and White.

When your child won't listen to you, other authority figures are lifesavers. When my kids think I'm a dingus, sometimes a coach, teacher, or neighbor can straighten them out.

Sometimes the behavior problem needs a physical solution. Have them do jumping jacks or run laps around the house. Sometimes logic fails and you need to reset their brains with some physical activity or meeting a physical need. Run them a bubble bath, make them a snack, or put them to bed. Sometimes it's purely physical. I know when my blood sugar is crashing, I need a snack, not a lecture. When I'm angry or stressed, I need to go to my Zumba class and dance it off or go stretch it out on the yoga mat. Both our kids and us parents need healthy snacks, regular exercise, and access to chocolate to keep from killing each other.

If all the usual tactics aren't working, don't be afraid to take them to the doctor for some medication, therapy, or interventions. Therapists can teach our kids, and us, helpful strategies, and doctors hold the keys to tweaking our brain chemistry. Everyone's concerned that we're overmedicating our kids, but let's don't throw out the prescription baby with the bathwater. Sometimes we cause more harm to our kids by denying them the medication and services they need. Get a few opinions, make your own decision, but if your child's behavior problems go beyond simple discipline, trust your instincts and assemble a team to help. You are a good parent, and sometimes good parents need to call in the professionals. Avengers, assemble.

No matter what your kids get into, figure out how to love them through whatever it is. Draw them closer, rather than push them away. Keep the relationship intact. That doesn't mean ignore the thing. Ask yourself, "What's the loving thing to do here?" The overarching goal of discipline is to build the relationship. Within a trusting relationship, a lot of the behavioral issues work themselves out.

I generally think I'm doing okay because on any given day, at least one of my kids hates my guts with a fiery vengeance and at least one thinks I'm amazing, and it changes regularly. Late one night, my daughter told me I was a cool mom, but by the next morning I was the worst, and I'm honestly not sure which assertion worried me more. I like to dazzle them with my hardassery and surprise them with grace. Keeps them on their toes.

Every time I say, "Here's how we do things," I'm very aware that all it takes is one person to say, "Actually, your kid operates an underground crime ring and you're the most clueless parent on Earth." I mean, I don't think my kid is doing that, but I can't be a hundred percent sure?

Your Kids Will Be Idiots

Whether you want to admit it or not, your kids will be idiots on many levels, whether they're shoving something in an orifice, sneaking somewhere, or breaking something. You might spend an exorbitant amount of time worrying they're going to get themselves killed. This is normal.

When I was pregnant and having my tenth meltdown about [pick a toxin] in [pick a product], my mom told me, "I feel sorry for your generation. You know too much." She had the luxury of raising kids in the 1970s and 1980s when they just focused on the people in front of them and didn't know about every kidnapping, paraben, or speck of gluten in the world. It was a simpler time. I remember spending all day running around the woods near our house, getting covered in mud from head to toe, and playing on the railroad tracks. My mom would ring a dinner bell as the sun started dipping down and we'd race home, strip in the garage, and hustle to the table for a delicious casserole featuring cream of chicken soup. We were total idiots, but no one worried too much about it, because we didn't have the internet feeding us a continual stream of panic-inducing clickbait. If my parents panicked about anything, it was whatever Focus on the Family told them, which is why I was never allowed to play Dungeons & Dragons. I don't think it affected my spirituality, but it did probably save me from being an even bigger nerd than I already was. (Sorry, fellow nerds. No disrespect. I already had glasses, zits, and braces, played the viola, and read Shakespeare for funsies. D&D would've been the kiss of death.)

These days, we can't embrace the natural idiocy of childhood because we're deathly afraid everything will kill our children, or worse, they won't get into Harvard. We think the world is less safe than when we were kids, so we tighten the reins until our kids can't breathe. There's a stranger lurking around every corner just waiting to snatch our babies.

Our perception of a scary world isn't even true. The world is safer than ever, but we have access to more information. In *How to Raise an Adult*, Julie Lythcott-Haims shares that "FBI statistics show the number of missing persons of all ages went down 31 percent between 1997 and 2011." Lythcott-Haims concludes,

"Terrible things happen everywhere in the world. But terrible things have always happened, and they are statistically less likely to happen today than in previous decades."[2]

We can lighten up and let our kids experience the world around them. And I promise you that they'll be idiots just like we were. Continuing to breathe when observing your kids is really the key. Oxygen is important. My youngest likes to climb to the tippy top of any tree or swing set, and if I ask her not to climb so high, her go-to reaction is to climb even higher. Monster.

When observing your kid doing something death-defying, breathe. And blink. Remember to blink. Your kids will go places you don't want them to go and they'll chomp things you don't want them to chomp, like you're living a real-life game of Ms. Pac-Man, and you hope it's the cherries around the corner and not the ghost.

At some point they're going to eat something weird. Don't panic. You know that line in *Tommy Boy*, "Did you eat a lot of paint chips when you were a kid?" My son ate whole board books as a kid, so the answer is yes. I found myself trying to look up where the paint on the *Bob the Builder* books came from and was it or was it not lead-based (he's fine; nobody panic), and when I say that he's a voracious reader who devours books, I mean that in the fullest sense. He began his reading career literally eating books, and by second grade read the entire *Harry Potter* series in a month. So, who knows? If your kid ingests books, maybe he'll end up with a huge vocabulary someday. (Look for the sequel to this book, *Eating Your Way to Literacy!*, coming to a bookstore near you.)

My youngest is probably part goat, chomping on paper and

---

2 Julie Lythcott-Haims, *How to Raise an Adult* (New York: Henry Holt, 2015).

even swallowing a penny on her birthday. I called the nurse hot-line at the hospital and then we were on penny watch for several days, poking through her poop until it came out the other side. Parenting is so glamorous.

Quiz

Your kid poops out money. Do you:

a. Throw away the money because ew.

b. Disinfect the heck out of the money and put it back in your purse.

c. Put it in the little "Give a Penny, Take a Penny" tray at the store.

We totally did whichever one you chose because I want you to like me.

They chew pen caps, drawstrings, sleeves, straws. If it's at all malleable they'll find a way to sink their teeth in. At one point I bought therapeutic "chewelry" for everyone, these necklaces that they chew on purpose. It didn't work, because my kids need to participate in illicit activities, and somehow being allowed to chew the thing rendered it totally unchewable.

When they're not shoving things in their mouths, they're shoving them elsewhere. Pick an orifice, and a kid has shoved something in it.

One day when Evie was younger, she was having trouble hear-ing and said her ear hurt, and when I shined the flashlight on my phone down into it, I saw what looked like a shiny hot-pink bead.

Me: Honey, did you put something in your ear?
Her: No!

Me: Are you sure?

Her: Yes! I didn't put anything in my ear!

Later that day, I picked her up from school and took her to the doctor where we waited with all the flu viruses swarming around us. Listen, kids, if you're going to shove things in your ears, please wait until after flu season. It's only polite. I slathered hand sanitizer all over myself after touching the office pen to sign the credit card slip. The "reason for visit" they listed on the sign-in form? "Foreign object in ear." I do think the pink bead was made in China, so I guess it really was foreign. It wasn't a domestic bead.

They called us back, and the doctor tried to look in her ear. Evie blanched, and the doctor offered, "Why don't I start with the ear that isn't causing you problems?" Okay. She looked inside and said, "There's a bead in that one, too." So, her good ear also had a bead in it. Then she looked in the ear we came for. "Yep, there's a bead in that one, too."

Me: Hey, Doc. Does this look like an accident?

Doc: Not in both ears. Maybe if it was just in one, but both?

Evie: It was an accident! I didn't put beads in my ears! I had an itch in my ear.

Me: So, a pink plastic bead somehow stuck to each finger, you got itches in both ears, you went to scratch them, and matching beads simultaneously got shoved down inside both ears at the same time?

Evie: Yes. That must be what happened.

Me: Uh-huh.

Two nurses came in, one to squirt water in her ears to flush the beads out and one to hold the water-catching bucket. They squirted and squirted and both beads popped out, along with a generous amount of earwax.

We thought we were done. The doctor came back in to check her ears once more.

Doc: I bet you're feeling better! Now don't put anything in
    your ears anymore.
Evie: I didn't put anything in my ears.
Doc: (*checking Evie's ears*) There's another bead in here.
Evie: I didn't do it!
Me: Not one, not two, but three accidental pink plastic
    beads. Wow. What are the odds.

The two nurses came back in, and this bead was buried exactly in the middle of Evie's brain. It wasn't coming out. They flushed and squirted and flushed and squirted and finally it popped out, along with more earwax.

We thanked them and headed home, Evie still adamantly denying her role in all this, and I tried to explain to her that either scenario is problematic, whether she stuck the beads in and was lying about it, or if she truly was so careless and unaware that three beads somehow rolled into her ears and lodged there. Either situation did not inspire confidence.

Your kids are going to make mistakes, which may land you in the doctor's, principal's, or [insert authority figure's] office. The biggest challenge, in addition to figuring out and hopefully surviving the consequences of those mistakes, is keeping yourself from making even bigger ones by freaking out all over them and grounding them for the rest of their lives. My husband and I are classic overreactors.

Saying Sorry Doesn't Have to Be So Hard

I tell myself over and over, "Do not enter into the crazy. Do not let them drag you down with them. Rise above. Do not make this personal." This pep talk to myself works about fifty percent of the time, when I've had enough water, I'm not currently hangry, and one of the Hemsworths is massaging my neck while crooning about how pretty I am into my ear. The other fifty percent I feel my temper rise, my tongue assume strike mode, and my words unfurl out of my mouth. Where's a Hemsworth when you need him?

Yes, your kids will be idiots, but, and I hate to break this to you, so will you. Nobody told me when I became a mom, I'd have to be so wrong all the time. Probably if I was doing a better job, I could avoid some of this pain, but I just keep messing up. With all the arguing going down in my house, inevitably one of us says the wrong thing, and so often it's me. It's one thing for a teen testing out her boundaries to haul off with some spicy talk, but it's a whole 'nother thing when a forty-something woman does it. Sometimes I horrify myself with my lack of control. I spew forth like Mama Vesuvius.

If, like me, you screw up a lot, saying sorry will become a life skill. Learn how to apologize well and teach your kids how to do it. The nice thing about having to apologize all the time is that you're modeling how to do it for your kids. I mean, that's the whole reason I mess up. For the teaching moment, of course. My parents used to apologize to me when they made a mistake, and it was one of the most powerful, memorable things about my childhood. Seeing the strongest, biggest people in my life draw themselves down to my level and ask for my forgiveness made me realize that anyone can do it. No matter how much power you wield, you might mess up, and when you do, the best thing to do is own it and apologize immediately. How much better would our world be if leaders learned to apologize?

You will spend the rest of your life apologizing. So, you might as well practice. Evie made me a poem for Mother's Day:

> *Roses are red*
> *Violets are blue*
> *Sugar is sweet*
> *And so are you.*
>
> *You're the best mom*
> *You're always calm*
> *Maybe. A bit.*
> *I wish you a Happy Mother's Day.*

For the times I'm not calm, may I always apologize.

Don't Give Up. Lighten Up.

I had a conversation recently with one of my kids about a trouble area I was seeing and told them, "You need to practice self-control in this area. If you can't practice self-control, then I will have to practice parental control. I don't want to do this. I trust that you can do this yourself. What do you think? Do you want to use self-control, or do you want me to use parental control?"

Since the goal of parenting is turning them into adults who can make wise choices and regulate themselves, as our kids mature, we look for opportunities where they can start practicing managing their own lives.

They can learn how to calm themselves down. They can learn how to reset and try a do-over. They can learn how to course correct. And we want them to practice these tweaks while they're under our roofs.

You'll lighten up as they get older. Your youngest will do things you never would've let your oldest do at that age. You will horrify yourself. When my first kid was six, I wouldn't even let him play in the driveway by himself, and let's just say that when my last kid turned six, I wasn't even looking out the window. You get less judgy the older your kids are. I can only assume what we'll be okay with by the time they're in college. I choose to think this is because we're getting wiser, not because we're giving up.

Figure out what rules you really want to focus on with your kids, and depending on the kids, you might have to work on one at a time until they get it and are ready to move on to the next. We come at our kids with so many parameters; it overwhelms them when all they hear is no no no. Try to say yes as often as possible and save all the critical stuff for the big rule you're working on.

I began parenting each of my three kids at different ages. When I started parenting my son, he was an infant, and we had all the developmental stages to work through sequentially. With my youngest, we started at two, so we had a lot of catching up to do. With my oldest, we started at nine. It's impossible to instantly train a nine-year-old in everything they need to know to successfully navigate their new environment. You have to start simply and build. No matter what age you're parenting, resist the urge to overwhelm your kids with too many rules all at once. Maybe you start with "Use respect" (if they're yelling), or "Gentle hands" (if they're hitting), or my go-to, "Obey the first time" (if they're arguing).

You might have one kid who's a rule follower and makes you think you're a reasonably adequate parent, but chances are at some point you'll have a kid who wants to take your pretty mold and shatter it. When you have a fighter, ask yourself, "What's worth a fight?" Pick your battles because everything is a battle, so which battles matter to you? For me, it's not clothes. Or bathing.

One of my kids purposely wore mismatched clothes for years. Someone would give us a brand-new coordinated outfit, but we'd never get to enjoy that outfit. We'd see the top paired with clown pants, the bottom paired with a dirty shirt with a hole in it. When this kid started wearing two different shoes, I thought I'd lose my mind, but it was a season, and eventually the season passed. The kid experienced the natural consequences of being a weirdo, friends making comments, and uncomfortable feet.

As for bathing, I had a sit-down with one of my stinkos a few years ago and negotiated a shower schedule.

Me: You need to take a shower every other day.
Kid: Once a week.
Me: Three times.
Kid: Twice.
Me: Twice a week, and we renegotiate at puberty.
Kid: Agreed.

My kids were never really into cleanliness in elementary school, but the good thing is we also didn't have to worry too much about lice, because those bugs go for the clean-haired kids.

Thankfully, their resistance to showering evaporated come middle school. Nobody wants to be the stinky kid. (For more on this subject, look for my next book, *Girl, Wash Your Crack*, coming to a bookstore near you.)

Tenderized Parents

Whenever I speak at an event, I run into those parents, the seasoned ones, although I'm not sure *seasoned* is the right word. More like tenderized, as in with a meat mallet. After my cute little talk about parenting, they wander over to me, clear their throats, and say something about remembering those early days when the kids were little. We lock eyes, and I know. They've seen some action. Things have gotten hairy at home and they're smiling on the outside but looking around at the younger parents bouncing babies thinking, "Run away!"

If we were in a movie, it would cut to the next scene, where we'd be out back smoking in an alley by the dumpsters, croaking in our chain-smoker voices, "They don't know the horrors we've seen. But they will soon enough."

As parents, most of us will have those incidents that feel ginormous. I've had a few already, and I'm sure there are more to come. Things will happen that knock the breath out of you, and you'll wonder how you'll go on. But you will. It'll feel impossible. The fear might overwhelm you. You'll lie in bed all night, mind racing and stomach churning, trying to solve a problem that feels too big. It'll consume you.

But you'll get up the next day and the next. You'll keep loving your kids through whatever it is. You'll take it one step at a time.

You'll learn to lighten up about the thing. You'll all heal. (Probably. I mean, I don't know your life.)

20 IDEAS FOR GETTING YOUR MONSTERS TO BEHAVE

1. Keep discipline simple. Focus on one thing at a time.
2. Have them do jumping jacks or run laps around the house. Use physical activity to reset their brains.
3. As your kids get older, treat them like boomerangs. They ask to go somewhere, you say yes, and you release them out and then watch them come back. If the boomerang doesn't come back on time, or the boomerang takes a side trip, tighten up a bit and bring them closer to home for a while.
4. Bribe them, aka "positive reinforcement." What do they want? Find the carrot you can dangle and dangle it hard.
5. Take away a privilege, like a toy, time with friends, screen time, or their phone.
6. Allow natural consequences to play out.
7. Chores. Help yourself while helping them.
8. Serve a sibling.
9. Write lines. Have them copy out "I will not____" or a proverb or scripture from your holy book of choice.
10. Have them write an apology letter to the person they hurt.
11. Make them pay. Literally. If they break something, they earn the money to pay for it. If your kids miss the bus, make them pay for a Mommy Uber ride.

12. Try lowering your voice instead of raising it. Freaks them out. When they mess up, don't overreact in a way that's worse than their actual crime . . . ask me how I know.

13. "Obey the first time." I say this a lot.

14. Draw them closer, rather than push them away. Keep the relationship intact. Ask yourself, "What's the loving thing to do here?" The overarching goal of discipline is to build the relationship.

15. Let the unimportant stuff slide. Does it matter if their socks match?

16. Use fewer words. Resist the urge to lecture. Keep the explanation simple.

17. When your child won't listen to you, other authority figures are lifesavers: a coach, teacher, or neighbor.

18. Video them throwing a fit and play it back to them with commentary like *Mystery Science Theater 3000*.

19. Pour them a bubble bath, make them a snack, or put them to bed. Sometimes it's purely physical.

20. Trust your gut and seek out professional help if you think something else is going on.

3

Talking Is Hard

Lighten Up About Words

> "You think you're bold? You think you know sin? You're
> still learning the language. I wrote the bloody book."
> —*Penny Dreadful*

One evening my kid dashed over to me, barely suppressing maniacal glee. You know how you can tell when one kid wants to tattle on another and you can sense the juiciness of the crime by how excited the sibling is to get to you? I could tell whatever the kid was about to say was high on excitement. I started mentally preparing myself for how much it was going to cost.

"[OUR BELOVED SIBLING] is standing in the front yard screaming, "F*CK YOUUUU!!!" at the top of their lungs! And it's so loud I could hear it from my room upstairs!"

Okay, first—whew—there's been no property damage, and no one needs the hospital. But relief was temporary when I discovered that our next-door neighbors had invited a family over for dinner that night and the timing was horrifically perfect. As our neighbors were welcoming this nice family into their home, our ruffian next door was standing in the front yard screaming F*CK YOU.

Our next-door neighbor is a pastor. Our pastor.

We don't even try to fake it anymore. I just hope this incident, along with pretty much every other day ever, will reserve us a permanent spot on the pastor's prayer list. We could use all the help we can get.

We spend a lot of our parenting energy worrying about words. We worry about whether or not our kids will talk in a timely manner, and then when they finally do start talking, we worry about what they're actually saying. My son hardly spoke for the first few years, and we panicked about that, but now that he's grown, we panic about what might come out.

My oldest spoke Russian when she first came to us, and we learned to parent with hand gestures and depended heavily on Google Translate, which, as you know, is extremely accurate all the time. Over the years, she mastered English, but now we're on the downward slope of the parabola as she communicates solely through emoji texts and TikTok videos.

My youngest loves to yell loudly about race and process her feelings about being the only black person in our family at the most exciting moments, like in the middle of Target or when I'm the only white person in the room. Until I learned to lock the bathroom door, she was also a fan of bursting into the room unannounced, then describing how "Mommy has hair down there" to anyone who would listen.

Now that my kids are getting older, we spend basically twenty-seven hours a day talking about the f-word, who's saying it, who wants to say it, why they shouldn't say it, and how they wish with all their hearts they could say it over and over.

In addition to the embarrassing things kids say, you have the things you're supposed to say and not say. All the books and articles tell us what to say and what to never say, but I find the wrong things coming out of my mouth over and over. And in the wrong way. I promised I would never yell at my kids, but I yell all the time. Today I thought I'd pop a vocal cord; I was yelling so loudly. Words are hard. Should we just stare frozen in place, afraid to utter a word? How do we calm the heck down about language?

"Look at That Lady!"

"That man is *smoking!*" my child gasps, horrified. She learned in school that smoking kills and she wants to go let that man know right now before it's too late.

Maybe you're walking in the mall one day, and your adorably observant child screams excitedly, "That lady has a face tattoo of Neil Diamond!" After panic-sharting your yoga pants, you respond, "Aren't people interesting? What do you like about it? Would you get a face tattoo? Should we be kind to her?" (Yes, jackass. The answer is yes.)

At some point in your parenting career, your kid will use their outdoor voice to make an observation in public. When it happens, remain calm. We've all been there. It can be an opportunity to teach them about treating everyone with dignity and respect.

Kids don't have our decades of experience giving nuanced levels of appropriate side-eye to the people around us. They're direct and unapologetic in their casual observations and make you want to pretend like they aren't yours and you have no idea whose rude kids are flapping their mouths off in Sam's Club. Their worldview is so teeny tiny, and they aren't used to seeing anyone who looks differently than whatever you have going on up in your home, so everything is weird to them.

Come to think of it, this is also true of some adults who need to expand their universe a bit, give a front hug to Black Jesus, and recognize there're lots of people in this world.

Strangers come up to us all the time and make comments or ask us questions. "Are you their mom? Are you the nanny? Are they all yours? Are they your *real* kids? Are they your *own*? Are they siblings? Where are they from? Was she in an orphanage? Did her real parents die?" I used to walk around smiling to counteract my resting-bitch face, but between the invasive questions and a guy flashing me his full twig and berries on my way to lunch last year, I'm letting my RBF shine relentlessly upon the overcurious passersby.

I grew up people watching. It's fun to watch other people walk by and make up stories in your head. I call this creativity and teach my kids to do it. *What do you think they're up to? What's the story behind that couple over there?* Make up stories about people all you want. Just don't tell them about it. You and your kids can spend ten minutes concocting a fun teleplay about why I'm at the post office dressed in my nightgown. (Answer: Thought I could pull it off as a tunic top. Couldn't.) Spend all the time you want figuring out my story, but then resist the urge to come up to me afterward and say, "I just have to ask . . ." No, you don't. No one is making you ask. Dig deep and find some self-control.

Start Early with the Hard Conversations

When Elliott rode next to his new baby sister in the car the day after we brought her home from Ethiopia, he looked at her legs next to his, him in his booster and her in her car seat, and exclaimed with astonishment, "Mom! Our bodies are different colors! Hers is brown and mine is . . . is . . . is gray." Gray? Okay, maybe he needed a little iron in his diet. He was four years old, noticing race for the very first time, and thus began a lifetime of talking about race, racism, sexism, and really all the -isms.

Avoiding these conversations doesn't make them nonexistent. And I'm mostly talking to my fellow white folks, because people of color here in my home country of the US of A are very aware of race and racism, and it's the privilege of white parents that we can raise our kids pretending race doesn't matter.

Over the years, we've spent a lot of time at the dinner table talking through current events, newsworthy items, things happening at school or on the bus, correct terms for different kinds of people, and how we defend the rights of everybody.

My kid saw a white friend use a racist word on social media and gently let her know that wasn't okay and asked her to take it down, explaining why, and they had a really great dialogue about it. This happened because we've been having these conversations for years, undoing some of the stuff they come home from school with, challenging them on things they've heard, and talking about everything from racist words to systemic racism.

Same goes for sexism, ableism, homophobia, and religious discrimination. Kids come home with questions, and we need to have safe, open dialogue about this stuff as they get older. My kids have asked if gay people can be Christians because they heard on the bus that they couldn't; they've asked about everything from Muslims to Mormons, and we keep teaching kindness and love and sticking up for their classmates.

Is that fair? Is that right? How would you feel if someone treated you that way for who you are? How do we show that person love? Hashtag WWJD. And if my kid is on the wrong side of something, we unpack that together.

These conversations are ongoing, and the older the kids get, the more often we're reading books, watching videos, and working to be more respectful and inclusive as a family. Develop relationships with people who are different than you. Let your kids see you cultivate a widely varied set of friends. Let them see you learn new things and humble yourself to other people's points of view. Don't shy away from the important stuff. Please don't raise your kids to be colorblind, because the world isn't colorblind, and our kids deserve a complete education from us. And other people's kids deserve an educated community.

Hamilton Taught My Kids the F-Word

Your kids will experiment with spicy talk. Don't freak out. Because we have to teach them how to communicate, at some point they'll pick up some new material. Maybe from you, or maybe from my kids at the park, who are most definitely trying out some stuff.

I'll never forget being a faux-edgy junior higher who was dying to bust out and do something crazy but felt the heavy weight of conservative Christianity pressing on my modestly covered shoulders. I was cleaning my closet one day, and a box fell down. I stared at the box. I formed the word in my mouth, and I said, "Shit." Then I decided I wanted my mom to hear me say it. I needed her to hear me. So, I yelled it louder. "SHIT." I waited in bug-eyed anticipation. I heard her down the hall yell back, "I HEARD THAT," and I felt simultaneously exultant and ashamed. I knew what my mom thought, I wasn't sure what God thought, but I was thrilled.

Swear words are cathartic. There's something delightful about forbidden language, and I have no problem with those words, with one exception. I love swearing, but because of my fundamentalist upbringing, I will pull the van over and rip my kid a new one about blasphemy, or as we grew up calling it, "taking the Lord's name in vain." But all the nonreligious swears get a pass. Don't you BLEEPING #@!?# take the Lord's name in vain.

I'm not 100 percent sure what qualifies as taking a name "in vain," but I think it has something to do with saying a name in an offhanded or derogatory way. They'd better effing respect the shoot out of our Lord and Savior. But sometimes they don't, and I honestly have no idea what to make of it. My inner child waits for lightning to come streaking down from the sky or Hologram Jesus to appear crying in front of us, but my loosey-goosey adult self figures God's probably all, "Simmer down, you adorable recovering legalist."

I love swearing, but I try to lock it down around the kids so they have a fighting chance of not being sent to the principal's office. The other night at dinner, my son said, "Daddy swears, but Mommy doesn't ever swear, so Mommy is better." (Nobody tell him Mommy is a pottymouth. It's our secret.) We spent an entire dinner discussing the f-word, its uses, and which kids in the neighborhood are saying it.

Kid: I really want to say that word. All my friends are saying that word. I'm dying to say that word.

Me: It's just a word, but if you say it at school or around certain people, or maybe at the office someday, you could get sent to the principal's office, your boss could fire you, or people might judge you and leave you out of things. Learn self-control.

Actually, *Hamilton* taught my kids the f-word, not me or Alex. I'll never forget picking Ana up from fifth grade for an appointment and right when she got in the car, Hercules Mulligan dropped his most perfect of f-bombs in "Yorktown (The World Turned Upside Down)." She looked at me and said, "Oh THAT'S the f-word. I wondered what people were talking about."

And I sheepishly replied, "I'm listening to *Hamilton*. About the Revolutionary War. It's educational." And then we drove away while Hamilton and his crew won the war and wrote the Federalist papers.

Don't worry about the swears. Focus on kindness. I'm less worried about the edgy words they experiment with and much more concerned with whether or not their words are kind. And they might suck at that, too. It's a learning process, and sometimes we have to learn the hard way, own the consequences, and apologize.

I never underestimate the importance of a well-timed swear, but I tell my kids if every other word out of their mouths is an f-bomb, then they're not living up to their creative potential or using the full spectrum of language. I feel this way about bad writing and lazy comedians. We have so many fabulous words to choose from, so vary it up a bit.

I also warn my kids that if they don't consider their audience, they'll make the wrong impression, because even if they don't care about the words, some people do, whether it's an employer or a teacher or a friend's mom, and some people will judge them based on the words coming out of their mouths. To everything there is a season.

So much of parenting is teaching your kids to read the room and be socially acceptable. More than anything else out of my mouth, I find myself murmuring at them, "Lock it down." Lock it down, people. Hold the crazy in and wait till you're home to unleash it.

This goes for farting, too. You know I'm right. How many times have you eaten a burrito at Chipotle and couldn't wait to get home so you could handle the cauldron of fury happening inside you? Some things we have to let out at home, and the sooner our kids can understand that, the better. And some of us have kids who will never understand that, so we need to hope for graceful fellow shoppers at the Walmart and get out of there as quickly as possible.

I'm a Yeller. Send Help.

At a recent family meeting, I asked my kids, "If you could pick one thing for me to do better when it comes to parenting, what would it be?" I knew what they were going to say, and sure enough, all three of them declared, "Stop yelling."

In my defense, at least 75 percent of the time I yell it's so they'll hear me over the volume of their own yelling. But yeah. Guilty as charged.

My mother is perfect in every way except she also yelled sometimes when we were kids, but she was mostly perfect. (I'm sorry, Mom. Please still buy this book and give it to your friends.) As an adult with perspective, I discovered that she was mostly yelling at our wacky dog Zak, who loved to jump up on the counter and eat everything within reach. The occasional time when Zak was on her last nerve and my insolence pushed her beyond the realm of control, she'd let loose with some healthy screaming. I swore I'd never yell at my own kids, which lasted for a whole two seconds until they learned how to walk, started destroying my house, and screamed at me all the time.

I yell. I'm a yeller. And honestly, it's not even usually because I'm mad. It's just that if I want to get my kids' attention and be heard over the dull roar of our home, I have to raise my voice, project throughout the house like I'm summoning the power of Grayskull, and probably repeat it five or six times.

Also, sometimes I'm mad. Kids know how to push all our buttons and stare unblinkingly at us with twisted little grins as they flick the final toggle that leads to our demise. Our emotions are a game to them.

Blog posts that tell me I shouldn't yell make me want to yell. I feel certain they're written by people with different temperaments or different children than I have. Some people say that screaming is bad. I call it "being expressive." If I bang my hip on the corner of the kitchen counter, a simple "Oh dear, that was quite painful" won't do.

In my quest to stop yelling so much, I've had to separate out the mad yelling from the "I just live in a super-loud family" yelling. There's a difference. While I don't think we should strive for homes with angry yelling, and obviously verbal abuse is never okay, the act of raising your voice might be absolutely fine. We need to lighten up about the yelling. Every home is different. Some of our household cultures are louder than others, and we of the Loud Houses should not be judged by the quiet. If you're quiet and everyone in your home uses their indoor voices at all times, by all means enjoy that. And please invite me over to read a book in silence because that sounds delightful. But for the rest of us, whether because of sheer volume of kids or sheer volume of voices, calm down and don't worry about the yelling.

I do have one kid who is sensitive to yelling, so I try to approach this kid with a lowered voice. The problem is that child is also a little hard of hearing, so I end up yelling anyway after the child has asked "What?" fifteen times. But I should get points for trying.

Me: Honey, will you hand me that plate, please?
Child:
Me: Hand me that plate, please.
Child:
Me: (*gesticulating wildly*) The plate. Right there. Hand it.
Child:
Me: HAND ME THAT PLATE NOW!
Child: Oh my gosh, Mom, why do you always yell at me?!?

Because I don't want to scar my children, I try to keep my yelling firmly in the nonhomicidal, rage-resistant category. It's a journey. I'll start yelling, realize my voice is raised, then try to body roll out of it like "WHY DID YOU PAINT THE CARPET WITH GLITTER GLU-uuue let's get this cleaned up okie-dokie!?" I'm sure it's confusing for my kids, because I'll start a sentence full throttle, then downgrade and try to smile sweetly to offset the crazy eyes. It comes out looking chillingly sinister, but I think the overall effect is more Playful Carnivore than Psychopathic Killer.

If you're yelling all the time because you're angry, that's a different discussion and one we're going to have in the chapter on emotions. Take your anger issues and join me over in chapter 7.

Every Word Out of Your Mouth Is Wrong

If I listen to everyone's input and try to take the advice of every parent or writer out there, I can end up in a shame spiral, afraid to even open my mouth around my kids. Some blog posts tell me I say everything wrong and make me wish I didn't know how to read. "You're not supposed to give them too much praise, but you're supposed to encourage them," and "Don't call them 'bossy'—call it 'leadership,'" and "Don't say 'normal,' it's 'typical,'" and "Don't tell girls they're pretty, but make sure they have positive body image." Last week I told my kids they sucked, so that's . . . bad . . . right?

When my son turned about three, I remember thinking, *Oh my gosh, he could remember this someday*. Up till then, every time I made a mistake or said a careless word, I told myself he probably wouldn't remember. I'd be a perfect parent starting now, and he'd never know what a screw-up Mommy used to be. That would last for ten minutes, maybe, and then I'd mess up again. After a while, I realized I was going to keep screwing up and there was no magic reset button. My son and then later my daughters were going to be disturbingly familiar with my imperfections.

Now that they're older, not only are they familiar with my imperfections, but they regularly make fun of me for them. I seem to fall short in every conversation we have, and raising teens means coming face to face with the full spectrum of how dorky you really are. You are a hopeless dork-face and do not understand anything, and when you try to talk, you elicit eyeball rolls and embarrassed tongue clicks.

Since I can't say anything right, I just say stuff wrong and hope for the best. I figure that in my favorite relationships I'd rather communicate awkwardly than not communicate at all. Lack of communication is a one-way ticket to relational death. So, around here we keep talking, even if we're dorks, even if we have to stumble around a bit for the right words. If you say the wrong words, apologize and work to find the right ones.

Talking to kids is like writing. In writing, as Jodi Picoult says, "You can't edit a blank page."[3] This book had to start somewhere, and it started with a large pile of crap. (You might think it's still a large pile of crap, in which case I invite you to skip leaving me an Amazon review.) When you try to talk to your kids and it feels like every word out of your mouth is wrong, keep trying. Write it down first before saying it if you need to.

I was hanging out with Ana last night and things were going great until the wrong thing popped out of my mouth, and she turned bright red, and I realized I'd been stupidly awkward for the twelve hundredth time. But I apologized, and we laughed and lived to see another day.

Talking is hard. Stay calm and keep working out the words.

---

3 Melody Joy Kramer, *Novel Ideas*, NPR, November 22, 2006. https://www.npr.org/templates/story/story.php?storyId=6524058.

Tell your kids how much you love them every day and don't worry too much about the rest.

10 THINGS TO DO INSTEAD OF YELLING

1. Walk away.
2. Do "big face, little face." This was an exercise we did in acting class to warm up our faces. Stretch out your face, open your mouth, widen your eyes, then pinch your face together, squeeze your eyes shut, prune up your mouth. Repeat this several times. I like to end on big face so everything feels open.
3. Chug a bottle of water.
4. Swear into a coffee mug.
5. Lock yourself in the bathroom.
6. Sing a song.
7. Start laughing.
8. Break out your '90s dance moves.
9. Make up a poem or rhyme random words.
10. Clap your hands.

But What If I Want to Miss Part of My Kid's Childhood?

Lighten Up About Work

> "All work and no play makes Jack a dull boy."
> **—*The Shining***

Early in our marriage, Alex and I went through a fairly committed *Return to Me* phase, in which we watched the movie on VHS millions of times. Something about the winsome nature of Minnie Driver and David Duchovny's relationship appealed to our fresh young love. These days we're more excited to watch *The Shining* together, so the years have hardened us and I'm okay with it.

When you watch a movie millions of times, you can't help but quote it, and since no less than sixty percent of my conversations with Alex consist of movie quotes from everything from *Monty Python and the Holy Grail* to *Army of Darkness*, it makes sense that we'd throw in a handful of *Return to Me* quotes as well.[4]

My favorite line from the movie is actually kind of profound, when Minnie Driver's grandpa, played by the late Carroll O'Connor, says, "I'm blessed with work," in a lilting Irish accent. Alex and I repeat it all the time, butchering the accent but agreeing wholeheartedly with the sentiment. We are truly blessed with work. We love our work a lot, and in addition to paychecks and stuff, get a lot out of it.

I love my work, but occasionally somebody likes to point out that I'm a horrible mother because of it. An acquaintance came up to me one time and said, "It's so great that you're a writer. I've always wanted to write, but I don't want to neglect my kids." Yep, that's me, author-slash-negligent mother. Between the internet and real-life advice givers, I've heard it a lot: "You don't want to miss out on your kids' childhood." Such a good point, except, is it? Obviously, I don't want to miss the whole thing, but is it okay for me to miss parts? After all, it's their childhood, and I already had a childhood of my own. I missed my son's birthday one year so I could hear Nadia Bolz-Weber speak at a conference. (I'm sorry, Elliott. But she was a really good speaker.) Some people need to calm the heck down about the work-parenting balance.

It's funny, and I can't quite pinpoint the issue here, but I get questions all the time about how I balance my career and parenting, and Alex gets questions about that zero times. What could the difference be, hmm, I can't quite figure it out—oh! It's my vagina. It's hard to have a vagina AND kids AND a career without raising questions.

---

4 Bonnie Hunt directed, cowrote, and costarred in this movie, so all the snaps for female writer-directors.

Alex and I both work from home and share the load around here pretty fabulously, and the only drawback I can see is that we get no credit with our kids. They think we are the worst. Whereas other parents leave for work and benefit from an "out of sight, out of mind" mentality, we are never out of sight from our kids, and they're always extremely put out that we won't just watch a movie with them or take them shopping in the middle of the workday. Our kids exist in a constant state of disappointment in their neglectful parents. If we commuted to work, we'd come home at the end of the day like heroes, but instead our kids stare at us staring at our computers and assume we're ignoring them to play Fortnite.

On the positive side, we can throw in a load of laundry on our lunch break, and I'm currently typing this with my Maltipoo, Khaleesi, on my lap. And we save so much money on gas. No complaints. I love my work. Love it, love it. And I want to teach my kids to love theirs, too.

Your Work

Some of you depend on your income to pay the bills, whether you're a single parent, you and your partner both work, or you are the breadwinner in the family. *Breadwinner* feels like an archaic word, and I try to avoid wheat in general, so winning bread doesn't feel like a real motivator. Maybe we should call the people bringing home paychecks winewinners or air-conditioningwinners. Because wine and air-conditioning are both very essential to my well-being. Anyway, for some of us, the age-old work-parenting balance question is super moot. You work because you have to and would like to smack those of us talking about staying home with your breadwinning baguette. Choice is a privilege, and let's not forget it.

For those of us with the privilege of choice in this area, we spend an exorbitant amount of time deciding whether or not to work, how to balance work and parenting, staying home and working, leaving the house and working. We worry we'll miss something crucial to our kids' development and beat ourselves up about it. And some of us wish we could miss a little more of our kids' development because there has to be more to life than playing dollhouse for five hours straight.

I was raised by a stay-at-home mom who also worked part-time as a bookkeeper. She was my role model, and I wanted to be as good a mom as her someday if I ever had kids. Many of my friends are incredible SAHMs and love it and are committed to that daily hard work. They volunteer at the school on a regular basis, they love having a house filled with kids, and they tell me they truly feel committed to full-time parenting.

I am not like them. Part of me wants to be, but after trying it myself, I started worrying I'd end up on the news, "Georgia Mother of Three Staples Children to Wall and Flies to Aruba." I really, really sucked at it and had to find another thing in addition to my darling and beloved children. After a few years, I finally admitted that in my case, non-parenting work makes me a better mom and that staying home with the kids was the hardest job I ever had. I've become a bit of a hybrid as a work-from-home mom. Motherhood is put on this pedestal as the highest calling a woman could have, and it's great, but maybe your calling is being a kickass orthodontist who happens to have kids.

Parenting is incredibly important, but it doesn't have to complete us. I thought motherhood would totally fulfill me, but it doesn't. I love being a mom, and lots of other things, too. It's okay if you don't enjoy parenting all the time. It doesn't make you a bad parent. Perhaps many of us fall into the category of needing something else along with parenting, and it just depends on our financial circumstances, co-parenting situation, and personality types as to how involved that something else is. Some of us need to work full-time in addition to parenting, some of us need the occasional outlet for another skill set, and some of us need a part-time job or volunteer opportunity. I've had different phases of my life with all those options.

When I started writing and speaking full-time, I asked my kids, "When do you need Mommy the most?" and they unanimously agreed that they needed me right after school. When they first get home, they want me off the computer and up in their business, checking in about the day and getting them snacks. Of course, as they're getting older, they really would prefer that I stay out of their business entirely, but too bad—no takebacks, kids.

Obviously, it's a privilege that I can be around after school, and not everyone has that kind of flexibility with their jobs. So, within the parameters of what your schedule allows, ask your kids what time they think is the most important for them to be with you. Is it Saturday mornings on the couch or maybe bedtime snuggles? I give it my all from right after school through dinner, but then I peter out and phone in bedtime stuff. Maybe bedtime is your time to shine. It's helpful for us to know what time to prioritize and what time is okay to duck back into the office or smartphone and finish up a few things.

Even when my kids were little and I spent all day every day with them, I learned to schedule concentrated time with them and time to let them free play, which is a fancy way of saying, "Go find an activity on your own!" I'd give them a solid hour of my time, then get up and do what I needed to do for a while. Whether you work an additional job or the parenting thing is your main gig, learn to lighten up about this pressure to spend every available moment with your kids. You're their parent, not their BFF. Give yourself a break.

I love my work so much, but sometimes I struggle with a little mom guilt, especially when my travel takes me away for days at a time. What if my kids feel neglected? What if I'm spending all this time talking to other people about parenting while my kids resent my choices and plot to kill me? I've learned not to overschedule myself and, after a busy season, to take some time to be present at home.

This year, one of my kids wrote an essay for school that started with "My mom is my role model," so it makes it all worth it. Whatever our work is, whether we're full-time stay-at-home moms or dads, work outside of the home, or work from home, our kids are watching. I want my kids, especially my daughters, to see me working hard and loving what I do. I want them to see that they can chase their dreams. I want them to see that it's okay to be responsible for work, often to prioritize work, and to find purpose in what they do, even when it's hard and they'd rather be playing.

I think my son will be fine. Boys are taught that of course they'll have amazing jobs and get paid what they're worth and be allowed to prioritize work. But girls are taught mixed messages. Work hard in school, get great grades, but be content to give up all your goals to raise kids, and certainly don't expect equal pay. I want my kids to see that I value raising them and also that I fight hard for my dream job.

Dads Are Parents, Too

"You're so lucky Alex helps you with the kids."

"Alex is so awesome to let you go to that conference."

"Your husband is amazing for watching the kids while you work."

Yes, let's all give him a shiny trophy for . . . being a parent. He's not a freaking babysitter. He's their dad. If you're a dad reading this book, you are wonderful and I'm not belittling the work you do. You're fantastic, just like my husband. I don't have a problem with you—good grief, you're reading a parenting book. But I'm really rather pissy with other people reminding moms every second of the day to be grateful to you for simply doing a job you signed up for when you contributed the sperm.

Even here in the twenty-first century, we fight an uphill battle for equality and respect. I tell my kids often that girls aren't better, and boys aren't better. We're equal and deserve equal treatment. Alex and I went to the same college, but as soon as we graduated and started a family, he was expected to continue pursuing his dreams, and I was supposed to stay home.

One way we try to teach our kids about equality is by simply pointing out the times when things aren't equal. We have discussions around the dinner table and talk about the current problems as well as the history. We go to movies that display positive female characters. I don't take just my daughters. My son needs to see these just as much, maybe more, and he's learning to notice when something isn't fair and to say something about it.

Me: Kids, I'm taking you to a movie called *On the Basis of Sex*.

Them: WHAT?! You can't take us to a sex movie OH MY GOSH, MOM.

Me: It's starring the actress from *Rogue One*. About Ruth Bader Ginsburg, the Supreme Court Justice.

Them: A sex movie about Ruth Bader Ginsburg!? Why would we want to see THAT?!

Me: The title is misleading.

Moms, I don't know how you split up labor at home, but if you have a partner running around in there, you guys work out what your schedule looks like and don't feel like you have to grovel or apologize to anyone about it. For those of us who tend toward control freakishness, we do have to lighten up about how our partners parent. Sometimes my husband does things differently than I do, and I've had to learn to respect the way he parents. My way is not the only way.

Since my husband and I both work from home, we chuck our kid duties back and forth like a hot potato. I take the morning routine, he takes the bedtime routine, I handle food, and he handles technology. We both take homework, but secretly I try to get the kids to trust him with projects involving poster board or ingredients "because Daddy's just so good at the creative stuff." Don't tell him I said that. Seriously, guys, don't mess this up for me.

A study by researchers from Arizona State University and Oklahoma State University examining how the "invisible labor" of managing the household affected the well-being of American women found that nine in ten of the women participating in the study felt completely responsible for the organization of their families' schedules, even though 65 percent of them worked jobs in addition to parenting. Seven in ten of the women were also responsible for maintaining their families' routines and doling out chores, and eight in ten were the ones who knew their kids' teachers at school. This burden of invisible labor negatively impacted women's mental health.[5]

I don't know what the division of household labor should look like in your home, if you churn the butter and he wrangles the horses, or you sterilize the knives and she hides the bodies. If you're a single parent, then you're like, "Let's see . . . one parent . . . divided by one . . . equals I still do everything myself." If you have a couple of parents in the mix at your house, sit down and have a conversation about the division of labor. And it might change, depending on your current schedule. We have basic responsibilities laid out, who's in charge of getting which kid to which practice, who handles signing school forms, and who keeps track of where the checkbook is, but every week we have a quick meeting about who's responsible for what, and we offer to pitch in as needed. For instance, this week I'm finishing up edits on this book, and he offered to handle the morning routine for me. I told him I was fine, but the fact that he offered makes me feel supported as a parent. Last week he was crazy with work, and I offered to get Evie to soccer practice for him even though he's the official soccer parent in the family. Keep the conversation lines open and don't just assume "the mom handles this stuff."

---

5 Kimberlee D'Ardenne, "Invisible Labor Can Negatively Impact Well-Being in Mothers," Arizona State University, *ASU Now*, January 22, 2019. https://asunow.asu.edu/20190122-discoveries-asu-study-invisible-labor-can-negatively-impact-well-being-mothers.

Alex and I continually tweak who does what around here, because when we start taking each other for granted and making assumptions, one person will feel overburdened and, if that person is me, a little pissy about it. If I were a cat, I'd poop in his shoes.

Your Kids' Work

In any decently functioning group of people, everyone has a job to do, and a family is no exception. We work hard at our jobs, and so do our kids. I teach our kids that their job is school and depending on how much effort they put into that, they may or may not have more choice in their jobs after they graduate. They have their day jobs as students, and then they come home to homework, sports, and chores.

Just like our own work might have a few categories, like career work, volunteer work, and parenting work, so does the work of our kids. Our kids have school, chores, and if they're old enough, actual jobs with bosses and paychecks.

I'm sure my kids wish they got a paycheck for schoolwork, but they get something better: the privilege of a decently provided-for childhood and the confidence that someday they can move out and make enough money to do what they want, far, far away from our rules. Whenever possible, I try to point out to them when they're applying something they learned in school, because my kids tend to think it's all meaningless. Maybe you have a kid who loves school and lives for essay tests. My kids are not those kids. Whenever they complain about school, which is every minute of every day, I sympathize and remind them that school is their job. They have to go to their job, do their best, and work hard, but they don't have to like it. It's a transaction. They show up; the teachers impart wisdom. Their feelings have little to do with it.

The goal with all the school is to find something they actually do care about enough to turn into a career they like. And to help prepare them for that, we give them chores, which they never like. Chores suck, but they're important.

In her book, *How to Raise an Adult*, Julie Lythcott-Haims cites George Vaillant's longitudinal study of Harvard students that concludes "chores in childhood is an essential contributor to success in life." Lythcott-Haims goes on to assert:

> Even if our child's sweat equity is not needed to ensure the smooth running of our home, they must contribute, know how to contribute, and feel the rewards of contributing in order to have the right approach to hard work when they head out into the workplace and become citizens in the community. In short, chores build the kind of work ethic that is highly sought after in our communities and in the workplace.[6]

I remember Saturday mornings as a kid, my mom bursting into my room, flinging up the blinds, and singing the "Good Morning to You" song while clapping her hands loudly. My mother is of course perfect, but she is not known for gentle wake-ups. Most Saturdays, I'd awaken to loud singing and this:

Mom: Melanie! (*clap clap clap*) You've slept long enough! (*clap clap clap*) Get up! (*clappity clap clap clap*) There's a list of chores downstairs on the kitchen table!

---

6 Julie Lythcott-Haims, *How to Raise an Adult* (New York: Henry Holt, 2015).

I'm not sure if she was looking to inspire me with the chore list thing, or if it was more of a threat, like "Get your butt downstairs or that list will get longer." But I was a fairly compliant child and shuffled downstairs to groan my way through sorting laundry, Windexing mirrors, and other tasks that seemed cruel and unusual at the time and are now things I do every day.

My mom was consistent but also did all the heavy lifting around the house, as evidenced by the phone call I made a couple of years into adulting.

Me: Mom! How do I clean a shower?

Mom: How have you been doing it for the last few years?

Me: Badly. I have this daily shower spray, but it won't take all the black stuff off the grout, and the bottom of the shower is turning brown, and it won't come off.

Mom: Do you own anything with bleach in it?

Me: No.

Mom: How did I not teach you this?

Me: I think you were concerned with quality control. Also, my childhood was awesome. Thank you, Mommy.

My kids have it better and also worse than I did. We have a glorious housekeeper who comes every other week to scrape a layer of dirt off the house. If our budget ever got too tight to afford her, I would rather give up food than my beloved housekeeper. So, my kids don't have to do a lot of vacuuming and dusting. But they do have daily chores, and I hold their screen time hostage on Saturday mornings until they get their weekend lists done.

The younger you start the kids with chores, the easier it is, because for some weird reason little kids think helping Mommy clean is fun. One year for Christmas we gave Elliott a singing broom and dustpan, and he thought it was the greatest. By the time they're old enough to figure out that cleaning sucks, it's too late and they're conditioned.

If we're going to activate our kids' latent abilities to pitch in, we're going to have to lighten up about the results. At first their chores feel more like chores for us as they spend fifteen minutes rolling around on the floor to fold one washcloth. I discovered this beautiful truth: you can't hear the whining if you leave the room. If you're a perfectionist who likes things done a certain way, letting your kids take on housework might drive you berserk. First, learn to let things go and encourage them where they are. And second, it's okay to go back and redo it once they leave.

When Ana joined us at age nine, she did not appreciate finding out about my chores. I don't blame her. Chores are terrible. But over time, with me ignoring lots and lots of pushback, we eventually fell into a routine. Now, she empties the dishwasher every day like a champ, and all my kids handle their own laundry. They bring it down to the laundry room, either they or I wash it, depending on if they're tall enough to reach the machine, and they carry the clean clothes upstairs and shove them into the mostly correct drawers.

Notice I didn't mention folding. That's because I gave it up. There's no point. I used to force them to fold everything, but then the second they went into their drawers, they jumbled up everything anyway. So, we cut out the superfluous folding, which cut out the superfluous whining. And don't come at me with the Marie Kondo vertical folding where you can see everything in the drawers. My kids are clothed every day. It's fine. Everything is fine. Wrinkly and fine. It's okay to skip steps. No one can tell what's inside a closed drawer, and I relish my ignorance. Calm down about the folding.

Does the laundry get washed with the undies still attached to the pants? Maybe. Do I find random dishes in unexpected places? Occasionally. But things get done, my kids develop a work ethic, and I get a freaking break, so I call that winning.

I don't know what chores are like in your home, but for mine, I looked at what I needed done on the regular and fleshed it out accordingly and age appropriately. We try to pile on just enough to make the house go round without slaying our kids' spirits completely. I break chores into three categories: daily, weekly, and random helpfulness.

Daily Chores

The daily chores happen, well, every day. Each kid is assigned one, and it's just the thing they contribute to the good of the family.

Ana puts the dishes away, Evie's in charge of spraying and wiping down the kitchen table and chairs, and Elliott folds the thousands of towels in our house. At first, he doubted his ability to fold a towel with any acuity, but now he's a towel-folding champ, and all it took was several weeks of me threatening his precious video games. I taught him to fold and roll the towels, and every day I find a neat little pile of towel rolls good enough for display in a fancy hotel room waiting for me.

Speaking of towels, this is just me, but I think we need to lighten up about towels. I know lots of families have beach towels, pool towels, bath towels, and the gross towels for bathing the dogs, but we just have towels. I tried the whole monogrammed thing and different colored towels for different bathrooms, and it was a hot mess. I don't have the bandwidth for color-coded, personalized towels, so we just grab whatever. Lighten up about towels. It doesn't matter. Unless it matters to you, in which case please carry on and enjoy your towels that match your bathroom wallpaper. Just don't judge me when you come over.

Weekly Chores

The weekly chores include cleaning rooms, cleaning the garage, and doing laundry. These are also just jobs they do because everyone contributes to running the household. On the weekends, you'll find me standing in the kitchen pointing to piles of various school stuff, sports stuff, toys, and half-finished craft projects while the kids race around collecting their crap and putting it where it belongs.

Honestly, how many cheese stick and yogurt tube wrappers can one family accrue? I'm constantly flabbergasted during our weekly digging out that we have so many. I'm actually not sure what surprises me most: that I find so many wrappers strewn about or that none of my people know how to throw them away on a daily basis.

Random Helpfulness

Random helpfulness could strike at any moment. If they're near me and I need something done, I'll ask, they'll sigh dramatically, then they'll accomplish whatever the task is. And next time they'll remember to go find an activity and stop complaining of boredom around me. I want my kids to develop the ability to pitch in, to see a need, maybe even a need that doesn't affect them directly, and help out just because it's the right thing to do. Certain kids are more wired for this spirit of helpfulness than others, but I try to cultivate it in all of them.

They've discovered over time that refusing to pitch in when asked or complaining about it will earn them more opportunities for helpfulness until they learn to hop up and help in a more timely, cheerful manner.

> **Kid**: There's nothing to do.
> **Me**: Fold these towels.
> **Kid**: Never mind. I thought of something.
> **Me**: Great. You can go do it after you fold these towels.

Sometimes people worry that they're overburdening their kids with too much work, and sometimes they overburden themselves trying to create the perfect chore chart with the right balance of jobs to motivational stickers. We've tried charts in the past but have found that for our family they aren't sustainable over the long haul. If charts help you organize and motivate your kids, then great. If not, lighten up about the charts and focus on daily and weekly chores and cultivating a general spirit of pitching in as needed.

Money Money Money

There's one more category we use in my home: chores for money. If my kids are trying to earn money for something, we have a list of chores and how much we'll pay, things like washing baseboards, weeding the flowerbeds, leaf-blowing the yard, sweeping the back deck, cleaning and vacuuming out the cars, and cleaning the basement. These bigger jobs earn cash for video games and makeup. We used to include "neck massage for Mommy," but the overall quality was lacking, and my kid tried to overcharge me.

When my daughter became a teenager, I told her I'd invest in her babysitting career by paying for her to take the online Red Cross babysitting course. Once she presented us with the certificate of achievement, Alex made her business cards, and I passed them out to all my friends. She started babysitting around the neighborhood, as well as dog-sitting, and she's really good at it.

When they get to high school, make them get a job. We are just at the beginning of this part, so I'm not going to say too much, because that's like when newlyweds write marriage books and I laugh at them and say demeaning things. But our oldest just turned old enough to be employed and get paychecks, and it's teaching her about answering to an employer, earning money for hard work, and that ever-important horrified gasp when you see "FICA" on your pay stub and wonder who he is and why he took your money.

22 AGE-APPROPRIATE CHORE IDEAS

You may be asking, "Should I let the toddler sharpen knives?" Great question. No. Here are some things we do for chores. If you live on a farm and your kids have been mucking out stalls since they could walk, feel free to snort derisively at the suburban fairy tale in which I'm raising my kids.

Little Kids

1. Pair up socks (and it teaches them matching!).
2. Wipe kitchen table and chairs.
3. Dust.
4. Wipe down baseboards.
5. Straighten their toys.

Medium Kids

6. Windex windows and mirrors they can reach.
7. Rake leaves.
8. Sweep the porch.
9. Wipe down the bathrooms.
10. Weed the flowerbeds.
11. Put away their clean clothes.

Big Kids

12. De-turd the yard.
13. Empty the dishwasher. (I pulled the scary knives first until they were older.)
14. Use the leaf blower.
15. Wash and put away the laundry.
16. Clean out the refrigerator.
17. Organize drawers and cabinets.

Teens

18. Babysit and pet sit.
19. Mow lawns.
20. Power wash the driveway.
21. Cook dinner.
22. Go get a job!

5

Can Everyone Please Notice How Awesome I Am?

Lighten Up About Yourself

> "If I had known the world was ending, I
> would've brought better books."
> —*The Walking Dead*

I knew something had shifted when *Harry Potter and the Deathly Hallows* came out and I found myself reading it in fifteen-minute increments per boob while nursing my son. It's one of his favorite books, so nobody tell him that his copy is covered in Mommy's breast milk.

I remember on the weekends when I used to read books all day long with no interruptions, just because I could. Kids came, and life changed. My schedule changed, and my me time changed from me time all day to I can't even poop without a kid on my lap or change a tampon without a kid asking me forty questions through the door.

As we learn to lighten up, the most important category may be lightening up about ourselves. Our kids barrel into our lives and everything changes. One day you wonder, *What should I do today?* and then you have kids and twenty years go by before you get to wonder that again because every day is Keep Them Alive Day, and it takes everything you have.

After you have a kid, the first time you get invited to do something and you can't—or you try but end up in the bathroom pumping breast milk the whole evening—you feel like your world is ending. Is this what it is now? One day you're living your life, and the next it's the zombie apocalypse.

The way you spend your time changes, and the way you see yourself does, too. One second, you're dining at a place where the waiter says, "Let me explain how our menu works," and the next, you're scarfing pancakes at IHOP before your kids start throwing scrambled eggs at the lady in the booth behind them.

I used to be kind of cool. Well, that's a stretch. I was never cool, but I felt at home in my clothes and never worried about spit-up stains on my shirt when I tried to leave the house.

I'll think I'm pulling this thing off until I open my van door and trash falls out and my kids are screaming at each other and cracking jokes about balls. We will never, ever look cool, and the number one thing I've had to do is calm down about what people think of us. I'd say I'm 70 percent there. Maybe 65 percent.

I remember we had to keep our voices down when I was young so the neighbors wouldn't hear our crazy. My mom would hiss, "Melanie. The neighbors," and I would feel properly chastised and lower my voice. My kids only have one volume—crazy loud—and I'm a yeller, so, I mean, the neighbors know.

Just when my kids got old enough to stay home by themselves

and not cover me with viscous fluid on my way out the door, just when I started to reengage with culture and feel like I know stuff again and poke my head out of the fog of early childhood, just when I started to feel sort of cool again, my kids developed their own taste in music and fashion and remind me every day how uncool I really am.

"You're wearing THAT?!?" my daughter shrieks on the regular. She also likes to comment about how I could use some Botox and how the wrinkles around my mouth don't go away after I smile. Feels good.

Yesterday my son called me a "saggy old lady" and told me I was bad at Legos. I'm not sure what's worse, his name-calling or questioning my nerd cred.

"This saggy old lady will destroy you at Legos," I muttered threateningly.

I'm tempted to go back to bed, but I'm learning to lighten up about myself. I have to, because middle schoolers can be cruel.

Hey, parents, we have to calm the heck down and stop taking ourselves too seriously, because when our kids aren't toying with our greatest fears, they're embarrassing us in public. It's too bad after delivering the placenta, we can't immediately grow thicker skin.

Parenting: The Most Embarrassing Thing I've Ever Done

As an overachieving people pleaser, all I've ever wanted was for people to think I'm doing a good job. All I've ever wanted is for people to think I'm doing the best job anyone has ever done in the history of jobs. But from the moment I became a parent, my visions of grandeur got hazy, partially because parenting has revealed my total inadequacy and partially because my kids give zero effs.

Soon after moving to a new region of the country, I took my brand-new baby shopping for a practical, microfiber sofa that would hide dirt, hopefully with some kind of antimicrobial finish on it to keep us from growing a petri dish situation in our new family room. As I was explaining all this to the nice saleslady helping me, we, along with several other women jaunting through the store, were enveloped in a stench of death. It wasn't a poopy diaper. It was a pants apocalypse.

My son was going through a phase where he only pooped once a week, and when the time came, No Diaper on This Earth could contain it. He liked to time these events to coincide with trips out of the house. I liked to use cloth diapers. It was a dark time. Obviously, I bought the sofa because after what we did to that store, I had no choice.

Twelve years later, that couch has been through so much. But it had an inkling from the start what it was in for. And its microfiber fabric still hides all that we can throw at it. (Look for the sequel to this book, *Parenting with Indestructible Furniture*, coming to a bookstore near you.)

Shockingly, when my kids grew up and learned to talk, the embarrassment continued. Kids say the darnedest things. When Ana was in the fourth grade at a new school, I volunteered to speak at career day. New Girl's mom was a published author. Not too shabby. I pulled together my notes on everything I'd learned about writing and publishing a book. (I only had the one, so it didn't take long.) I had to bring her younger sister, Evie, who wasn't in school that day. Evie nestled herself crisscross applesauce on the gym floor, surrounded by fourth- and fifth-graders ready to hear my vast knowledge. At the end of that thirty seconds, I asked if anyone had questions, and Evie's tiny hand shot up.

Good humoredly, I called on her, and she blurted out loudly, "Mommy pulls her pants down and pees in the yard." Lies. I would never. But the ten-year-olds in the gym didn't know that, and my Q and A session was over at that point. I didn't realize I could still die of embarrassment in front of a bunch of kids, but yes, yes, after thirty years, elementary schoolers are still intimidating as frick.

As they get older, the stakes get higher and the public humiliation grows exponentially. After all, we've come to expect toddlers wigging out in the toilet paper aisle at Target, but when your older kid tells her teacher that you don't know how to cook dinner, drink whiskey for breakfast, and never hug them, you wonder when child protective services will come a-knockin'. (These things aren't true. These are examples. Shut up. You don't know my life. Wait—what have you heard?)

The great news about embarrassment is that right when you can't take one more public meltdown about shoes, they mature enough to realize that other people can see them and they have a reputation to maintain. At this point you have a few options. Try to stay as invisible as possible around their friends. Say nothing. Breathe quietly. Avoid loud patterns or neon colors. Drop them off several blocks from where they actually need to go. Or. It's payback, baby. Threaten to roll up to their school blasting "Bohemian Rhapsody" and drop it like it's hot when chaperoning the school dance. Payback is a bitch. Usually, I don't even actually need to embarrass them. Threats are enough. If they pop out of line, usually the first few bars of "I'm Too Sexy" will do the trick.

Strategies for Dealing with Public Humiliation

Reconcile yourself to never being cool again. Because really, a parent trying to be cool to their kids is actually kind of the saddest, most uncool thing, and it's hard for the rest of us to watch. Rather than trying to hang on to some semblance of pre-parental coolness, focus on developing strategies for dealing with public humiliation. Because it's inevitable.

If your kid embarrasses you or you embarrass yourself, the first option you have is the *Monty Python and the Holy Grail.* Run away. It worked for King Arthur with that dreaded rabbit of doom. It's okay to leave your shopping cart full of stuff and race to your car. Or throw money on the table at a restaurant and race to the car. Or grab your kid kicking and screaming at a birthday party and race to the car. When things are going horribly wrong and your kid is throwing down, sometimes all you can do is get out of there.

This is why grocery delivery was invented. You thought it was for hungover people on Sunday morning, but it's for parents held hostage by their kids. And lest you think toddlers are the only ones who can throw down in a store, let me tell you that a pubescent twelve-year-old hell-bent on buying five-inch heels will also lose all reason in the shoe aisle of Target. Or so I've heard. Hypothetically.

The most important thing is that no matter what our kids are doing in public, we have to appear calm and in control. If we manage that, no one else will freak out. If we're firmly chanting, "Kids who scream in stores don't get ice cream" while smiling like a Stepford Wife and maintaining our yoga breathing, people won't panic. If we join our kids in Crazytown and scream back, everyone will worry.

I had a kid who would sit in the child seat of the shopping cart at the grocery store and try to bite my hands and kick me in the gut. So instead of praying for a personality transplant or investing in a Kevlar suit, I learned to push the cart from the other side while the gremlin swung its legs drunkenly at the air.

In addition to tantrums, you will also encounter wardrobe malfunctions. Once you become a mom, bike shorts underneath your dress will be your best friend. Never leave home without them, especially if parenting has left you little time to maintain your lady garden. Because kids love to treat skirts like parachute time in PE, you'll need protection when they're venting your special area in the middle of the church lobby. If you forget, you'll wish you had a commuter lane to Jesus.

Wardrobe malfunctions are inevitable when you have kids. When we first moved into our new neighborhood and our oldest came to visit us from Latvia, I took the kids to our community pool and introduced myself to the neighbors sitting around. Wanting to show off what an amazing parent I was, I began tossing Ana in the pool over and over, while she chattered happily in Russian, giggling *"rusalka,"* which means "mermaid."

Many, many minutes later, vast acres of minutes into this endeavor, I realized that the man I'd seen when we came in was staring fixedly at the fence. *Odd,* I thought. *What's he looking at?* I glanced down and realized, to my horror, that he wasn't looking at something. He was looking away from something. And that something was my nipple, which had wormed its way out of my bandeau top like a curious snail. Bike shorts under skirts and swimsuits with straps, unless you have the kind of sturdy décolletage that stays put under extreme duress. I do not. After a year of nursing, mine is more the malleable consistency of Moon Sand.[7]

I'm not sure what the dad wardrobe malfunction equivalent is, because you guys seem pretty okay with us all seeing your hairy man nips at the pool. Wait, I know. Because of the proliferation of ultra-baggy "dad pants," aka cargo shorts, your junk is safe from view, but not from impact. You might want to wear a cup, because I've seen some situations go horribly wrong. Nothing's popping out and making an appearance, but it looks like some kids really don't want siblings and are willing to make sure that can't happen. The Involuntary Vasectomy. Are you even a dad yet if you haven't been headbutted in the 'nads by a four-year-old pretending he's Juggernaut? It's all fun and games until someone loses a nut.

Do Something for Yourself Before You Give Up and Run Away

Parenting is this nonstop, exhausting, sometimes humiliating experience, and we have to calm down and take care of ourselves so we don't burn out. If you could break parenting into three phases—early childhood, elementary years, and teens—we're basically in a triathlon, swimming, biking, then running, so we gotta hydrate, hydrate, hydrate, and also pop those little energy gummies now and then.

As parents, we want to put everyone else first. We give and give, but we end up feeling depleted and resentful. People talk like

---

7 I told a longer version of this story in my essay "My Body Is Yours," in Ashlee Gadd, *The Magic of Motherhood* (Grand Rapids, MI: Zondervan, 2017).

it's a good thing to run ourselves ragged with the parenting, but it's not. Workaholism isn't healthy, whether we're talking about our office jobs or our parenting jobs.

Parenthood has become a religion, and people worship at its altar. The more we're self-flagellating for the sake of our beloved children, the holier we look.

"She stayed up all night handcrafting her elementary schooler's Thumbelina costume while writing her high schooler's college admission essay. What an amazing mom she is." Amazing Mom ascends to the next level of heaven and earns four gold crowns.

My road to parenting took me twelve years, multiple surgeries, and three continents. No one has to tell me these kids are important. They are so incredibly important. But they are not my everything. There's more to me than motherhood.

The first time I took my kid to the doctor and they simply referred to me as "Mom," nameless guardian of this child, I felt like Sandra Bullock in *The Net*, stranded in another country with my identity stolen, running around trying to convince people that I still exist. When I hang out with other parents, I like to bring up subjects that have nothing to do with our kids, to get to know people as individuals and not just "Nancy's mom."

We need to learn how to say yes to ourselves every now and then. Do not put your life on hold while you're raising your kids. Do not make raising your kids your whole life. Who were you before you had kids? Who are you apart from your kids? Find an outlet, find your passion, and keep at it, even if it's a small project you work on every night after they go to bed. For years, I blogged quietly in my closet, in obscurity, as a way of having something to show for my day. I wrote terrible blog posts, I helped get orphaned and vulnerable kids sponsored for Children's HopeChest, and then as my own kids went to school, I tapped out a writing career on my laptop.

We feel guilty about it, but we need to lighten up about the guilt. We have to keep cultivating our minds apart from parenting. Read books, go to museums and galleries, take walks outside if that's your thing. Do not lose yourself in parenting. It's too long a life phase to put yourself on hold.

Sometimes I go to therapy. Therapy is helpful for our kids, and a few years ago I had one of my kids' therapists tell me I should get myself back in with my own. *What gave it away, Doc? Am I coming across a little anxious? This is shocking.*

The number one thing I love about therapy is that it's a guilt-free place to talk about yourself. Anywhere else you're going to have a give-and-take, but not in therapy. You are paying an expert to listen and take notes about everything you say. With your partner, friends, and even your mom, you're expected to reciprocate and ask them about their lives. Or at least you should if you're doing the whole relationship thing right. We need a back-and-forth with healthy relationships, and when it's focused on the needs of just one person, it's going to suck the listener dry and eventually peter out.

But not with therapy. Nope, you can show up week in, week out, and make it alllll about youuuu. You're the star of your own YouTube channel on the therapist's couch. It's the You Show. And my therapist was even helpful in getting me to steer back to myself when I'd start to try to solve my kids' problems. I'd veer into their territory and start to make it about them, and my therapist would ask, "And how are YOU handling that stress? How is their problem making YOU feel? What can we do to help YOU as you carry that weight?"

Therapy can be different for everyone, and I do different things in different seasons of my life. Sometimes I drive to an office, but lately I've been seeing someone halfway across the country via video chat on my laptop. Maybe for you it's a spiritual advisor. Whoever it is, make sure it's a healthy experience and you're getting solid help from people with the right training and letters after their names.

Whatever it looks like for you, cultivating hobbies, finding your passion, or going to therapy, take a breath, take a break, and calm down. Learn how to say yes to yourself now, because this parenting thing is here for a while.

20 IDEAS TO SAY YES TO YOURSELF

The internet is always talking about self-care, but everyone defines that differently. I think we can all agree that we need to take care of ourselves, but we need to lighten up about what that looks like because it's different for each of us. Here are some ideas for a variety of people. I would never do several of the things on this list and maybe you'd never do a few that I love.

1. Spend a half hour in a hot bath reading a book.
2. Take on a new project that excites you at work.
3. Have a night out with friends and make your partner be your Uber service.
4. Sit at the kitchen table with a cup of coffee and a word puzzle, Sudoku puzzle, crossword, or whatever.

5. Snuggle with a fuzzy blanket or a dog or a heating pad.

6. Go to therapy and talk about yourself nonstop for a whole hour.

7. Go to an exercise class.

8. Take a walk. Open the front door and step outside.

9. Listen to the music you like, not the music you think you're supposed to like. I broke up with current music about a decade ago and decided to stick with Guns N' Roses and Aerosmith. I'm old, I like old music, and I don't care.

10. Read the books you want to read, not just the books you're reading to your kids.

11. Make a personal reading goal for the year. I read fifty books a year to absolve myself of the guilt of all the TV bingeing I do. Maybe for you it's one hundred. Maybe it's twelve, one book a month.

12. Buy geeky collectibles and arrange them on a "Wall of Geek." My wall of geek currently contains three Funkos from *The Walking Dead*, a *Star Wars* watercolor painting by my kids, *Doctor Who* Legos and tea set, a *Firefly* coloring book, *The Lord of the Rings* Pez dispensers, original film clippings from *The Lord of the Rings*, a *Walking Dead* viewfinder, and a plush goat head. These things make me happy, and my kids know these toys are off-limits or so help them Daryl Dixon I will go full Dalek on their butts and EXTERMINATE.

13. Book a massage.

14. Grab a friend and go to a thrift shop.

15. Color or paint a picture. At a girls' night a few months ago, we went to a pub and my friend brought her coloring book and colored pencils. I love that.

16. Plan a "creative arts" day. Go to a museum or gallery, get tickets to a musical, sit in a park and sketch trees, or listen to live music.

17. Have an adventure. Pack a bag and set out in your city for the day, ride public transportation, walk the streets, and people watch. Or if that's your normal day, then do the opposite. Set out for the country, roll the windows down, and buy fruit from a roadside stand.

18. Write a poem or essay.

19. Take yourself to lunch.

20. Sing karaoke by yourself. (Yes, this is the second time I've mentioned karaoke. Karaoke is an important part of my self-care routine.)

6

Sleep, Eat, Poop, Repeat

Lighten Up About Bodily Functions

"Whatever you do, don't fall asleep."
—*Nightmare on Elm Street*

The day we brought Elliott home from the NICU I realized I was scared of my baby. I was sitting in the dining room eating dinner that my mother-in-law had made. After spending six days myself in the hospital trying not to die, then commuting back and forth for another four days to hold and nurse my incubated preemie, we were finally all home together. I wished the NICU nurses could've come with us. I was exhausted and nervous, and my C-section scar was a mess.

I didn't realize how messy it was until a couple years later when the lady doing my bikini wax saw it and yelled, "BUTCHER!" If I were in a horror movie, she would've made the sign of the Cross on her chest and looked out the window at the flapping bat lit up by the full moon. My uterus and vicinity had been mauled by a demon.

So, there I was, sitting at the table, eating my mom-in-law's food, and staring fixedly at the cream-colored vibrating chair contraption humming on the floor at my feet. My four-pound babe was nestled in there, and I stared at his beautiful closed eyes, willing them to stay closed for a little longer while the chair lulled him to sleep, like the harp with Fluffy the three-headed dog in *Harry Potter and the Sorcerer's Stone*. I was terrified he'd wake up and rob me of my dinner. Elliott and I had a lot in common those days. All we both wanted to do was eat and sleep, but only one of us got to do those things.

I spent my days trying to get him to sleep, and then several years later, I repeated the whole process with Evie, except she was almost two, very mobile, and extremely loud. This was before the days of video surveillance features on baby monitors, so I perfected the army crawl in and out of their rooms to check on their breathing and sniff the air to see if they'd pooped.

Bodily functions are a part of life, and we become obsessed with what and how often our babies are sleeping, eating, drinking, and pooping.

"My baby slept through the night at four weeks old" could get you throat-punched by another parent. We spend an exorbitant amount of time wondering why they won't sleep, until they become teenagers and we wonder why they won't wake up.

Yesterday I made an emergency pharmacy run for my neighbor with a sick baby, and as we hung out and I reassured her that all would be well, she asked me what my parenting style was when I had a baby. Uh . . . medium? I employed the "hit a happy medium" style? My style was somewhere in the middle between all the styles. I read a book about putting your kid on a schedule, and the schedule was too strict for us. I read a book about not scheduling and turning yourself into an all-access human pacifier, and that was too loose for us. So, we meandered somewhere in the middle of that, having a schedule but not dying by the schedule.

I love hanging out with my neighbor. You can feel so isolated at the beginning of your parenting journey, and more so for her as an immigrant far from family and unaccustomed to the weird ways of American parenting. It's an honor to get to answer her questions about motherhood and reassure her that everything will be okay and that she's not alone. Yesterday I told her I have my own set of older moms reassuring me the very same thing, except with a whole different, teenage set of concerns. We all need people further along to help us navigate our current stage.

The challenges never go away; they just morph to the next thing. When they're little, we're so concerned with sleeping, eating, drinking, and pooping, and when they're older, well, we're still kind of just super concerned about all that. When they're little, you worry about what they're drinking, and when they're older, you also worry about what they're drinking and is it legal? When they're little, you want them to sleep, and when they're older, you want them to wake up and you go from quietly rubbing their backs to desperately yanking them out of bed for school.

Whatever stage of parenting you're in, remind yourself that this thing that seems so monumentally important right now will be a blip on the radar in a year or two. I'm talking about the typical life stuff, of course. Obviously, there are exceptions to this. Some things linger. We have some big things that aren't getting any smaller, but even with the big life things, you adapt over time. You'll think you're at the brink of despair, and then one day you'll look back and realize you made it and it's not all that. Kids will sleep, eventually. You'll figure out what they can eat, eventually.

Illnesses will come and go. The poop and pee will ebb and flow. Cue *The Lion King*, "Circle of Life."

Naps Are for Quitters

As a baby, after the first few months of nocturnal torture, my son took three glorious naps a day and still went to bed at 6:30 p.m. and slept all night. He was the greatest sleeper for a while there. Nowadays he stays up most of the night rereading *Ready Player One* and all the Harry Potter books, but as a baby, he was a snoozing dynamo. Even after he dropped that third nap, then the second nap, that afternoon nap held strong for several years. I took full credit. Clearly, I'd cracked the code on this sleep stuff.

Imagine my surprise when we adopted Evie, and she entered our lives like, "What is this *nap* of which you speak?" Naps were for quitters, and she wasn't having it. Instead of naptime, I told her she needed at least a quiet time, which was code for "Go to your freaking room so I can drink coffee and get my head on straight for round two."

Her version of quiet time and mine differed slightly. She felt like *quiet* meant screaming as loudly as she could for an hour until I came back to scoop her up and face the afternoon. I would've preferred that she play with Duplos or look at a book. To each her own.

Even now with big kids, I often send them upstairs for quiet time, especially if they've been out of line. They think it's punishment, but really, I'm saving their lives by giving myself time to cool off and regain a little sanity. *Go to sleep, child, so I can kill you in it.*

When the kids were little, they used to fall asleep in the car, and to this day, car rides often end in naps, but not on accident. Just getting through a six-minute car ride with my kids can feel like *Zombieland*. By the end, I wish I was a zombie and could eat them all and be done with it. Containing children in a mobile metal box and transporting them down the road takes more magic than I have.

The arguing and fighting and screaming are bad enough, but when they start to get physical, that's when things really ramp up. And the older they get, the more their wingspan increases so that even when properly belted in, they can reach their siblings to wreak havoc. To encourage our children to keep their hands and feet to themselves, we've instituted the Naptime Divide. The space in between their seats is the Naptime Divide, and should they choose to cross it with a wayward limb, foam sword snuck from home, or wadded-up spitball, they will receive immediate naptime when we get home.

Can you make your teenagers take a nap? No, you cannot. But you can take away their phones and send them to their rooms for an hour. The Naptime Divide cuts out the "She's touching me," "I'm not touching her" conundrum in which one child holds their hand precisely two millimeters away from the other child's eyeball. Is she touching him? No, that is accurate. Is it uncomfortable to have a finger two millimeters from your eyeball in a moving vehicle? Yes, yes, it is. The Naptime Divide is the buffer zone, our own Demilitarized Zone, and as the kids get older, I'm thinking about investing in some land mines.

"But how can you know for sure if people are following the rules while your eyes are on the road?" you ask. My kids, who may have a future in law enforcement, keep me informed of one another's movements at all times. They are their own neighborhood watch. This leads to charges of, "Mommm! She's crossing the Naptime Diviiiiide!"

Everything in Moderation

"Everything in moderation." Of all the parental sayings, I think this is my favorite one. My parents drilled it into me, and now I drill it into the next generation. It most often applies to food choices, but it's really just a good life lesson in general, unless we're talking about murder or heroin, in which case I find that a definite hard pass is a better call.

Throughout your tenure as a parent, you will come across many different ways of doing things that involve the words *always* and *never*. Always do this, never do that. Most everything that comes at you can benefit from an "everything in moderation" mentality. Or a "Not now but maybe later." "Not now" doesn't mean "Not ever." My mom always said, "We'll cross that bridge when we get to it," and that's some good advice. So, remain calm, take one bridge at a time, and practice everything in moderation.

We're such an all-or-nothing society. We love extremes. Either we barely stand up from our desk chair or we join some kind of gym program involving the word *shred* or *camp*. Either we don't own a TV or it's on all day. Lightening up means finding a balance. Moderation. Instead of "We don't do video games," maybe sometimes we do. Instead of "My kids aren't allowed to eat sugar," maybe sometimes they are. Parenting doesn't have to be an extreme sport. We can figure out what matters the most to us and relax a little about everything else.

I've had to relax a lot when it comes to food. I started out making homemade organic baby food, and these days I'm like, "Well, at least Nutella has protein in it?" We're supposed to mix up the food groups and get our kids to eat a variety of foods, but they tend to find one thing they like, like cheese or Nutter Butters, and then that's all they'll eat.

"Please eat a piece of fruit," I beg my kids. "If you eat that whole block of cheese, you'll never poop again."

We try hard, and usually in the beginning, we feel like our efforts are paying off. Then reality hits. One time I paid twelve dollars for a bag of organic apples that cooked down to a spoonful of applesauce, and then my kid ate a stranger's Goldfish crackers off the floor at Chick-fil-A. There's a slow slide from total control over every morsel that goes in their mouths to finding decimated bags of chips hidden under their beds.

When they start solid food, you worry they might choke, and the older they get, the more you'll have to be careful not to choke on your own food when they bring up stuff at the dinner table. *Did she just ask me what the c-word is in the middle of Taco Tuesday? Baby, the c-word is "cumin" and thanks for asking about the seasoning in tonight's meal.*

I read in a book that I could give Elliott chicken when he was nine months old, so rule-following new mom that I was, I took him to Chick-fil-A and bought him his first four-count nuggets meal.

I didn't even chop them up. I put down the handy plastic table cover—because I wanted my baby to have a sanitary place to choke to death—and plopped down four whole chicken nuggets in front of him, cheering him on as he gummed them and tried not to die.

It didn't occur to me until much, much later, while watching another mom carefully dice the nuggets into tiny morsels, that maybe whole nuggets were a bit much for a toothless babe. I'm really not sure how Elliott survived his childhood, but he's a real self-starter who learned to feed himself right out of the gate.

Food is nearly impossible at our house, and I'm hoping for space-age, Jetsons-style food pods to hit any minute, because raising three kids from three different continents means three very different palates. I've had to lighten up about dinner and do things like Potato Bar! And Build Your Own Rice Bowl! And This Is All You Get, So Eat It or Starve!

Just when you think you have a decent routine and have trained your kids to eat a variety of foods, they grow up and try to make their own choices. After talking with their friends in the school cafeteria or learning about trichinosis in science class, they develop Important Ideas and are happy to educate their stupid parents about the evils at the dinner table. Don't freak out, because most of it doesn't last. The other day Ana and I had this conversation:

> **Ana:** I was going to be vegan, but then I found out I couldn't eat Nutella, so now I'm a vegetarian.
> **Me:** I'm going to Wendy's. Want anything?
> **Ana:** The Baconator.
> **Me:**
> **Ana:** I'm a vegetarian starting tomorrow.

Everything in moderation.

My Kids Eat School Lunch, and No One Has Died

This week I had the culinary pleasure of attending my kids' annual holiday feast at school. At our school on feast day, we aren't allowed to bring in outside food. I think this is to encourage all of us to partake of the cafeteria delights and because they know we'd all bring Chick-fil-A and the cafeteria cooks who worked so hard would have nary a ladle to scoop. My husband and I grabbed our Styrofoam trays laden with ham, green beans, yams, and the holiday works, and scooted ourselves onto benches next to our kids. Was it Zagat-rated, Michelin-star-worthy cuisine? No. Was it a well-balanced meal? Yep.

Everybody freaks out about school lunch. We see the articles online teaching us how to create organic cucumber sculptures to nestle in recycled plastic bento boxes. We feel like we need to up our game in the lunch department. Listen, when my kids started school, I packed their lunches every day, but when more food started coming home spoiled and squished at the end of the day, and they were begging me for Doritos and Oreos like their friends ate, I decided to chuck it all, fill up their school lunch money accounts, and wash my hands of it.

Now they go through the line every day, and what happens with the food they buy is between them, their mouths, and the garbage can. Every now and then when they complain, I offer to pack their lunches, but I have a couple requirements. If you are in elementary school and want me to pack your lunch, you must ask me the night before by dinner time. I won't run around like a contestant on *Chopped* at 6:00 a.m. If you're in middle school or higher and want a packed lunch . . . do it yourself, darling. I will provide plenty of options for a lunch bag. Most of the time, they go with the school lunch, and really, it's more balanced than what I can scrounge up. I might manage some desiccated raw carrots if I pack a lunch, but the school lunch provides salad options, veggies, and fruit.

Lighten up about lunch. As my grandmother always said, "It only takes one filling." I'm not entirely sure what that means, but I think it's something like "Just get full on something," which from a woman who survived the Depression and is still kicking at age ninety-six, that's truly something to rejoice about.

You may be saying, "That's great, Melanie," and also, "Screw you and your dietary flexibility—nice wish." I hear you. I try to avoid wheat and dairy, and I'd explain why, but my agent says I should limit how many times I talk about diarrhea, and I think I'm already pushing it.

We went gluten- and casein-free with one of our kids for three years while we tried to work out some issues, and it was challenging. If your kid has dietary restrictions, you learn how to handle it and try to anticipate every situation. Zorya's mom is bringing in cupcakes for her birthday? No problem. You'll show up at the same time with an allergy-friendly version of the same cupcake that you stayed up till 4:00 a.m. baking after you got off work, nursed the baby, and binge-watched three episodes of *Game of Thrones* just to feel like a human person. I have been there, it's a ton of work, and you are amazing.

Maybe you have a kid who will literally die if they smell a peanut, and you hear other parents griping about how we aren't allowed to send in peanut butter sandwiches anymore and you want to throat-punch them. Some of our kids can't just eat school lunch or run through a drive-thru or trick or treat for any ol' candy. Those of us with dietary flexibility need to be inclusive of those needing more restrictions. We all need to do a better job respecting what other parents are dealing with. If your kid can't smell a peanut, then I can keep my peanuts at home. And if your kid can't have gluten, then we can playdate at a yogurt shop instead of the bakery. We can find common ground and respect our uncommon ground.

The Breastfeeding Illuminati Will Hunt You Down and Kill You in Your Sleep

My mom always says, "The pendulum swings too far," and that is the truth. Things tend to swing too far one way or too far another, and the darn pendulum never stops in the middle for any length of time. We are a people of extremes.

When I was a baby, my mom was a hippie freak for breastfeeding me when everyone else was using formula, and then when I had a kid, the pendulum had fully swung the other direction, where if you didn't breastfeed your child you were a terrible human being who should be publicly flogged. Ahem. We need to calm the heck down about the boob juice.

When I was lying in my hospital bed hopped up on magnesium and trying to get my blood pressure down, in between puking up ice chips and feeling like my entire body was on fire, I kept demanding a lactation consultant because, doggone it, I was going to breastfeed my son. I didn't get pregnant the way I planned, I didn't give birth the way I planned, but so help me Lord God of My Boobs, I was going to breastfeed my four-pound preemie.

I think actual flames must've shot out of my face when the lactation consultant proceeded to explain how I could pump and deliver my milk to the NICU so my babe could get his golden nectar. As soon as she started showing me the breast pump and I realized my eyes wouldn't focus, I knew there was a problem.

Since that experience, I've now been drunk enough to re-create that moment (just for book research of course), and it's when you try to focus your eyes, but they won't focus no matter how much you try to align them properly. My eyes kept crossing, and I spent the consultation honored that the hospital had sent not one but two lactation consultants. There was only one. I was just seeing double. They—she—was very nice and probably would have been helpful if I hadn't been drugged out of my mind. Maybe I'd rushed this thing a bit. Maybe I needed to do what the doctor said and focus on not dying. Maybe that was the best way to take care of my new kid.

The neonatologist wouldn't let me breastfeed Elliott until a full day off the sauce, I can't imagine why, and then when I was finally cleared, I pumped and pumped my boobies as hard as I could to produce . . . a smear of milk on the pump cups. The nurse generously offered to take the cups to the NICU, swab them off, and deliver the milk smear into my baby's mouth. Mmm, nutrients with a side of cotton swab.

After that humble beginning, we limped along with a combination of formula and breast milk for a couple weeks until I was finally able to sustain him on my own, but the weird thing is it never, ever comes up in conversation now. My closest girlfriends don't even know if I breastfed my kid. We never talk about it while shuttling our kids back and forth to sportsball practices. We're much more concerned with what's in the Crock-Pot and how many times we can run through the Chick-fil-A drive-thru before they cut us off. (If you weren't sure that I live in Georgia before, you can tell because of the number of times I've mentioned Chick-fil-A in this book. Y'all, it's right by my house.)

I have several friends who were never able to breastfeed, and the people around them made them feel like total failures. This is horrifying. We should be supportive of moms sustaining their babies any way they choose or any way they can. The kids'll be all right.

I adopted both my girls, and I don't even know if one of them was breastfed or not, and she certainly doesn't remember. I have friends whose toddlers are still motorboating them for a little nip and that's okay, too. It just doesn't matter in the grand scheme of things. (Okay, but if you're breastfeeding your teen before he picks up his date for prom, that's too far.)

We have to lighten up about how we feed our kids. The Breast-feeding Illuminati will not show up at your house and kill you in your sleep if it doesn't work out for you. Although if you wanted to and couldn't, I am sorry. I know that can be disappointing. I promise your kid will never know the difference. My mom's the smartest person I know, and she was a formula baby, and I was breastfed and well . . . yeah.

Porta-Potties . . . the Stuff of Nightmares

No matter how squeamish you are before you have kids, you will be elbow-deep in poop by the end of your first week as a parent. The shoot's about to hit the proverbial fan.

The number one thing I repeat around my house, more than

"Say thank you," maybe even more than "I love you," is "Wash your hands." I constantly chastise the kids to wash their hands. Don't even walk into my kitchen without washing your hands. When they enter the door from school, I greet them with "Wash the school germs off," and when we get home from church, it's "Wash the church germs off." Because everybody goes to church sick. Church is like an unholy petri dish. Every week when they force us to greet the people around us, I work so hard to avoid shaking people's hands. I grip my coffee with both hands, as if it's too heavy for just one, and if I try to let go to shake a hand I will fumble the mug and spill hot coffee all over you. I try hands in pockets. Sneezing on my own hands right before the shake and shrugging apologetically. Anything to avoid touching another human's disgusting germy fingers and clammy palms. I'm a super-loving Christian who just wants to love people from a three-foot radius. Forget "pass the peace." Try passing the hand sanitizer.

With this DEFCON 1 level of germ consciousness, you can imagine how excited I am having kids wandering around my house coughing on all the hard surfaces and wiping their noses on my sofa. At least now that they're older, they can wash their hands themselves and handle their own nose-blowing situation. And the bathroom. We're finally at that place where they don't need me in the bathroom.

"Wipe me!" would ring out like a little-kid version of "F*** you!" and I'd take a deep breath before entering the danger zone. Unlike Aaron Burr in *Hamilton*, I do not want to be in the room where it happens.

But I remember those days. They're fresh, like the pungent smell of a Porta-Potty on a hot day in Georgia.

Elliott swims year-round, but all three of my kids swim on our neighborhood swim team every summer, and it's one of my favorite things we do as a family. I love our neighborhood, and hanging out with my awesome neighbors cheering on one another's kids is the pinnacle of parenting fun. I'm not even being sarcastic, which is a stretch for me. I become the best version of myself on a pool deck cheering on goggled-up butterfliers dolphin-kicking their little abs off. I feel I'm at the top of my mothering game in June, volunteering for all the swim-related things and willingly getting up early each morning to get the kids in the pool on time.

Our team competes against the other neighborhood teams in our city league, and we spend Thursday nights visiting various pools around our town. One pool in particular has a difficult setup, because the only bathrooms available are of the portable variety.

Hundreds of wet kids. Hot summer evening. Soggy toilet paper. Aboveground raw sewage. What could go wrong?

When a certain child of mine was old enough to be on the team but young enough that I feel zero qualms about sharing this story, she ran over to me before her race needing to go potty. I sighed despairingly, looking at the row of Porta-Potties at the top of the hill, and we took off, hustling before they called her race.

We got to the tiny toilet, and I realized I'd need to help her, or she might fall in and end up swimming in a pool we had not planned for that evening. As I peeled her wet suit down her body, she steadied herself on the lip of the urinal, conveniently located adjacent to the toilet and coated in a glistening layer of male pee. I hissed at her not to touch the urinal, so she let go and grabbed onto my head instead, entwining her pee-pee fingers in my long brown hair. I love parenting. Parenting's my favorite.

About the time she settled onto the toilet with me holding her little body securely, I discovered that this was a Code Brown situation as a man-sized turd exploded out of her body, hitting the cesspool below with such velocity that it caused a geyser of poo to sluice into the air, spraying her naked back. At which point I heard them calling her race on the pool deck below.

But I am not a quitter. We are closers, and we do not back down from a challenge. I yanked her wet suit back up her body, gathered her up out of the potty closet, and hustled her down to her lane. As she jumped into the water, I thought, *Oh honey, take as much time as you want. You need all the time you can get in that chlorine after what just went down.*

And this is why leaving the house with kids is bad.

This child has stretched my germaphobe ways exponentially. This is the girl I found lying facedown, licking the ground at the airport. She sucked on the registration desk at the pediatrician's office during flu season. She ran her tongue up and down the checkout belt at the grocery store. And she's the healthiest one of all of us. This kid hardly ever gets sick. Her immune system has seen more action than a leper colony and has risen to the challenge. I fully believe she could fight off Ebola should the occasion arise. And if we ever encountered someone with Ebola, my kid would be the first one to greet that person with a full-body hug and a mouth kiss.

The great thing about your kids growing up is that you'll reach a day when you have no idea what their poop looks like. You won't even notice that it's happened. One day you'll be at their annual physical at the pediatrician's office and the nurse will ask the usual series of questions. When they get to the part about if their poops are regular, you'll look at your kid, shrug, and say, "I actually have no idea. Honey? How are your poops?" And your kid will widen their eyes in the universal sign for *MOM SHUT UP*, turn beet red, and mutter, "Fine." And that's when you'll realize you've reached the end of an era. A really gross era. Right when you pat yourself on the back, they'll get a stomach bug, vomit all over the car, and you'll be right back in it. Your fault, for partying in the end zone.

Vomit Rules

Speaking of vomit, after the Valentine's Massacre a few years ago, when one of my cherubs ate so much candy with red dye in it that they spewed it all over every item in the bed, across the bedroom floor, into the hallway, and through the bathroom, turning our entire upstairs into a scene from a Tarantino movie, I established Vomit Rules, a set of tenets we seek to uphold in our house. Before all the main candy holidays, Halloween, Valentine's Day, and Easter, I make the kids repeat the rules.

Me: I don't care how much candy you eat, but what are you not going to do?
Them: Puke.
Me: That's right. Know your limits. Check in with your stomach and make sure you're okay in between rounds. If you screw up and eat too much candy, where do you puke?
Them: Toilet, trash can, bowl, sink.

Me: In that order. Toilet is my preference, then trash can or bowl. If you can't make those, then hit the sink. The carpet is out.

Following last year's Post-Thanksgiving Minivan Debacle, after which I had to call an exorcist, aka a professional car cleaner, I added a rule.

Me: If you have to throw up in the car, what do you do?
Them: Ask you to pull over.
Me: If there isn't time?
Them: Grab a plastic bag or empty cup.

This is why you should never clean out your van too much. In our van, there's always an empty cup or bag.

Unfortunately, you can't always rely on the receptacles around you, so even the best planning can end in disaster. When Elliott was two months old, we Mary and Josephed our way from DC to Georgia. When we got here, there was no room in the inn, but my parents had a room over their garage, which we moved into temporarily until we could buy a house. Nothing prepares you for moving to Hotlanta in the summer and living over a sweltering garage with a newborn.

Elliott had an ultrasound at the children's hospital downtown a few weeks after we arrived, but the night before the appointment, I woke up vomiting and spent all night back and forth to the bathroom. You haven't lived till you've nursed a newborn while simultaneously offering Big D to the porcelain god.

When I came downstairs the next morning, my mom was finishing up her own dreadful night of it. We didn't know if it was food poisoning or an aggressive virus, but we were both afraid to leave the house for fear it wasn't over. My dad and Alex packed up Elliott in my parents' brand-new car and drove an hour to the hospital for the checkup.

As they pulled into the parking lot, Alex frantically motioned for Dad to drop him off, as the cauldron of fury burbled in his stomach. Whatever it was had hit him. He ran inside to find a bathroom while Dad parked with Elliott.

Safely inside a one-holer, Alex proceeded to decimate the bathroom, à la Drew Barrymore in *Santa Clarita Diet*. As he opened the door, a shell of a man, a young doctor started to enter, saw the mess behind, and veered away.

They made it through the appointment, got Elliott back in the car, and headed home. When the next wave hit, Alex grabbed an empty grocery bag that Mom had had the wherewithal to stash in the car just in case, and he puked and puked in the bag. Unfortunately, unbeknownst to anyone, the bag had a hole in it, and vomit started streaming out the bottom all over my parents' brand-new car, which was quickly losing its new-car smell.

Meanwhile, Elliott was screaming in the backseat, and they couldn't calm him down. Dad called us at home and told us to meet them in the driveway, exclaiming, "We're coming in hot!" We could hear Elliott screaming through the phone and could only imagine what we'd find when they pulled in.

As the car rolled into the driveway, we saw Dad's expression at the wheel, like a man who'd just survived a war. Alex was in the passenger's seat, wiping vomit off the seat belt, and Elliott, in his rear-facing infant carrier, was wailing hysterically. When we opened the door to get Elliott out of the backseat, we realized why he was crying. Left to his own devices, Dad had no idea how to strap a baby in one of those newfangled car seats with a five-point harness. So, Elliott rode an hour with his legs jacked up to his ears and the straps underneath.

There was nothing to do but die laughing, and to this day, if we have any kind of drama arise, we yell, "We're coming in hot!"

There's something about spectacularly gross situations that leave you no option but to find your sense of humor and calm the heck down. Vomit comes for us all, with no warning, so invest in a wet vac, breathe through your mouth, and scrub.

Feeding Your People

Let's talk about meal planning, because "speaking of vomit" feels like the right segue for that. Bottom line: to make it easier on yourself, plan ahead and keep it simple. I used to make fancy meals and enjoy trying new things, but then my kids learned how to talk and started complaining about everything. Food became this recurring nightmare where multiple times a day I was accosted by an angry mob demanding rations. I was pissed. One night I picked up my plate, stalked angrily into the next room, and ate dinner by myself.

Kids are hungry, hungry hippos until it's dinnertime and then they're Gandhi on a hunger fast. Every night at dinner they act like they've never encountered food before.

Them: What is this?
Me: It's chicken.
Them: What kind of chicken?
Me: The same kind of chicken you had last week. And the week before.

I even tried rebranding food.

"Tonight we're eating Happy Mini Trees (broccoli), Spaghetti Nuggets (tortellini), and Dairy Juice (milk)!" To no avail. Every inch of carpet in her room is covered in hair bands, Littlest Pet Shops, and used tissues, but my daughter will find the tiniest minced onion and turn her dinner plate into a CSI forensic lab with the tortellini cadaver laid bare.

"It looks like the noodle was murdered with a .002-millimeter piece of basil at 5:30 p.m. Apparently, the chef tried to (*whips off sunglasses*) spice things up." Cue the Who song and a boat whizzing through the Everglades.

Thing you never thought you'd have to say:

"Please stop eating napkins. Eat your food."

And then one day you'll fix dinner and your kids will eat it and say, "Mom, that wasn't bad. I sort of liked it." And you'll die with happiness. For a long time, finding foods all three of my kids would eat was impossible. Over the years I've managed to accrue a moderate list of acceptable foods, and I rotate the heck out of that list, occasionally stepping out of line and introducing them to something new because if I eat hamburgers one more time I will die.

I use a big ugly whiteboard on a wall in the kitchen to help prepare my kids emotionally for what they'll be ingesting throughout the week. On Sunday, I post the weekly menu. I started doing this not to be awesome, but out of self-preservation. After the four hundredth "What's for dinner?" of the day, you start to lose your grip on reality. It helps me, too, because by 4:00 p.m. I can't remember my own name, much less what veggie to start chopping. The whiteboard has become our dumping ground for pretty much everything we need to communicate. We keep track of chores and how much money they've earned, appointments and excursions, meals, and even guidelines for behavior. If my kids know they're having white bean chili on Wednesday, they can mentally prepare themselves all week. I get it. If I showed up to dinner hoping for pizza and got tofu kabobs instead, I'd complain, too. Mental preparation solves a whole host of problems and allows us all to lighten up.

Another way I minimize dinnertime whining is by reading to the kids. I got this idea from Jamie Martin's *Give Your Child the World*. She says:

> Bedtime reading isn't the only acceptable reading time . . . For years now I've found the best time for reading aloud to be during a meal—when little mouths are busy chewing, giving me a captive audience.[8]

I'm so wiped by bedtime that dinnertime reading has become our new normal. I've declared the dinner table a phone-free zone, so we can focus on time together. We've read *Wonder*, *A Wrinkle in Time*, Mark's gospel from the Bible, *American Like Me*, MLK Jr.'s "Letter from a Birmingham Jail," and biographies on Sojourner Truth and Harriet Tubman. My kids chomp chomp away as I get in a few pages every night. When they start to have side conversations and crawl under the table, I know it's time to stop.

Or you can hide in a closet and eat by yourself. No judgment.

Every Saturday I order my groceries online, which saves me so much money from all the impulse buys I used to grab, and every Sunday on our way home from church we swing through

---

8 Jamie C. Martin, *Give Your Child the World* (Grand Rapids, MI: Zondervan, 2016).

the grocery store parking lot, where a nice man loads up our car. Everyone helps me carry it inside, because big kids mean big arms and you can load those babies up, and then I head to the whiteboard to write out the menu.

I've had to let go of my culinary aspirations. Someday when we're empty nesters, maybe I'll enjoy complicated epicurean exploits, but this is not my decade for that. Taco Tuesday is a standing arrangement, and I mix it up different weeks with chicken tacos, pork tacos, or beef tacos, and provide an array of crunchy, soft, corn, and flour taco options for my kids' delicate palates.

My kids abhor veggies, so when I hear other parents talk about how much their kids love them and how you just have to expose them early, I roll my eyes so hard I'm a little worried they'll stick that way. I exposed my kids to veggies and various culinary delights throughout their childhoods. I exposed the heck out of myself. I was the exposiest veggie flasher that ever flashed her broccoli and carrots. (This paragraph is ending up somewhere else from where it started.) Didn't matter. When my kids reached a certain age, they were done and it became a game, except not a fun game, more like Michael Douglas in *The Game* game, and I might jump off a roof. (That's a spoiler, but in my defense, you had like twenty years to see that movie, so I don't feel bad.)

I've gone through various stages of playing the veggie game with my kids. Cutesy names, pureeing it and hiding it in their food, bribing them with dessert if they eat the veggies, sitting at the table for hours until they eat them, and making them go straight to bed if they don't.

I've learned to lighten up somewhat about the healthy food

situation around here. I dutifully present the healthy options, and they choose whether or not to consume them. At some point your kids will get too old to play airplane, and you literally cannot make kids eat something they don't want to. Try your best, then leave it to God and the Jolly Green Giant.

The meals my kids tolerate best are the simple ones with choices. They get a base, like potato or rice or shredded chicken, and then I have various toppings they can choose, like cheese, salsas and sauces, avocado, chopped and roasted broccoli, diced bacon, black beans, and so on and so forth.

Breakfast for dinner is always a win, whether it's bacon and eggs, pancakes, sausage and toast, waffles with toppings, or a combination. Serve with a bowl of fruit, hand everyone a banana, or blend up a smoothie. Done.

Friday night is Dab Night, a dab of this, a dab of that, named by my mother when I was a kid. It's that weekly time I force my kids to eat leftovers. Sometimes I call it Stewardship Stew and turn all the leftovers into some kind of haphazard soup. My kids groan. They hate soup, but once I explained that it's Stewardship Stew because we are stewards of the resources we receive and as such we shouldn't throw out a bunch of viable food at the end of the week, they came around and saw the efficacy of the stew night. Just kidding. They thought I was silly and made fun of me.

Dinnertime can still be problematic, but things have gotten a lot better, and cheaper, once I lowered my expectations, planned ahead, and kept it simple.

20 QUESTIONS TO ASK AT DINNER BESIDES "HOW WAS YOUR DAY?"

When the kids were little, we spent dinners just trying to get them to eat, not throw food, and sit up at the table. Actually, that's still what we do, plus add farting and burping. (At each meal, they get one gaseous freebie out either orifice. A second infraction costs them laps around the house. If you're reading this, my child, of course I mean your siblings and not you. You would never do that, and neither would I. Of course.)

We alternate with sharing highs and lows from our days, reading books, and asking questions. It's the one time a day I have a captive audience, so I try to take advantage of the twenty minutes or so. These days filled with teen drama, we spend at least part of most dinners debriefing about who threw food in the cafeteria, who broke up with whom, and which YouTuber said something stupid on the internet. My dad was always really good at asking questions and then letting me process my opinions and feelings about something, so I'm trying to do the same for my kids. Learning to ask the right questions takes time, creativity, and the ability to really listen.

1. Did anything smell bad today?
2. Did anyone say something funny?
3. What made you laugh?
4. What made you mad?
5. Share highs and lows.
6. Did anything weird happen?

7. Does anyone have a story they want to share?
8. Did you guys hear about this thing happening in the news?
9. What do you think about it? What do you think needs to happen?
10. If you were president, what would you do?
11. How can we help you this week?
12. What did you learn today?
13. What surprised you today?
14. What's stressing you out?
15. In the book we're reading, what stuck out to you in that passage?
16. Which character resonates with you the most?
17. Do you think the character made the right choice?
18. How would you have done it differently?
19. Have you ever had anything like that happen to you?
20. How does this story relate to what you're going through at school?

7

Mommy Needs a Time-Out

Lighten Up About Feelings

"You have no security system, Karen."
—*Halloween* (2018)

For the last two years, my word for the year has been *stay*. It's not like I'm a flight risk, per se, but sometimes everything just feels too hard. I'm at capacity, and then one more thing piles on and I don't know how to process it all and want to run away. I'll get frustrated and overwhelmed, but then something makes me stick around. I was going to give up on parenting, but then my daughter held my hand all the way through *Mary Poppins Returns*, and I decided to give it another day. Feelings swing back and forth, so I've learned to calm down and not to let them boss me around too much.

I knew that parenting would be physically exhausting. On top of the pregnancy stuff, I heard the stories about the late-night feedings and saw moms lugging five-ton infant carriers with one arm while balancing coffee. I felt relatively prepared for the strength training and cardio needed to parent.

I was, however, woefully unprepared for the psychological toll of parenting. I didn't know that my mental prowess would stream out through my breast milk. My son literally sucked the brains right out of me and left me unable to complete a full sentence without trailing off at the end wondering what I was saying, what day it was, and how to spell *the*. And I had no way of understanding both the privilege and enormity of carrying the weight of my children's emotions. Each stage of childhood brings a new minefield to navigate.

The other day I took my daughter shoe shopping. Don't ever go shoe shopping with a nine-year-old. As often as possible I simply present my children with their new shoes, or the older ones give me a link and I click, order, and render them unto their feet. But occasionally, when the stars align to say SCREW YOU, MELANIE, I need to take a kid shoe shopping, like when I can see the feet have grown but I can't tell how much. After agonizing over several pairs, she finally made her choice and said a tearful good-bye to the rejects. She cradled them in her arms, whispered sweet nothings into their laces, and in a final farewell, murmured, "Jesus still loves you." Good gravy, where do these deep feelings come from?

I cry about twice a year when enough junk builds up to finally blow through my sinuses like a freight train, but my kids are different than me, which is probably a good thing, so we go through a crap ton of Kleenex around here. I've had to figure out what I can handle and be honest about it. I'll hold my daughter for an hour or two, providing tissues and clucking sympathetically, but then at some point life has to move on, at least for one of us, so I tell her, "It's okay to be sad. It's okay to have these feelings. I'm glad you're processing them. I just can't process them with you anymore because I have to get dinner ready. So, I'm going to wrap you up in a fuzzy blanket, I'm going to snuggle you up with your favorite stuffed animal, and I'm going to walk over there and keep working."

Like Ross says in *Friends*, "Hug for her; roll for you."

My mom used to ask, "Do you want me to give you something to cry about?" I know that can sound threatening, like she's a mob boss or something, but she's hilarious and never meant it in a scary way. I actually wonder now what she would've done if I'd said, "Yes, yes, I would like you to give me something to cry about." Show me that movie *My Girl* again. That'll do it.

We all have various capacities for dealing with the emotional upheaval of our children. I'm fairly adept to a point, and then I hit a wall where I just can't handle any more. This is probably because growing up, my parents would give me one day to be sad about something and then I had to move on with my life. I wanted to tell my girl crying over the rejected shoes to get over it, but I sat there with her, grieving the shoes, like she was auditioning for *The Shadow Box*.

This is wonderful. Processing the emotions, so super important. I respect that a lot. Great work. Yay, empathy. And personally I need breaks sometimes, so I don't walk out the door and into oncoming traffic.

It's important to affirm our kids' feelings. I hate doing this. I want to shut the feelings down, beg them to suck it up, and move on. Instead, I say things like, "It's okay to feel that way. Feelings are important." Truthfully, feelings are exhausting, but depending on your children's personalities, you'll spend a large chunk of your life dealing with those feelings, so strap in and get comfortable with the idea. If you don't teach them to process their feelings now, then they'll just bottle them up and launch them at you at Thanksgiving dinner in thirty years. Might as well deal with them now.

What's Your Safe Word?

As the kids got older, started fighting constantly, and developed high-level arguing skills, I started to feel depleted in a different way than I did in the baby and toddler years. I felt like I was carrying the added weight of everyone's bad days, all the drama they encountered at school, and their triumphs and defeats.

I had to figure out a way to stay calm and rise above their emotional turmoil while still caring about them. I realized that I don't have to experience their emotions for them to matter to me. Their battles are theirs, and I can show compassion without entering into the melee myself.

Our kids will try to make everything our problem, and it's tempting to jump in and try to fix everything, but as parents, we get to choose which things are actually our problems to solve and which things aren't. When your kids are plummeting into big feelings, don't get down in the muck with them. Throw them a rope to help them climb out. I ask my kids, "How are you going to solve that?" Then I wait for them to answer.

The extraordinary thing about adulthood is that we've already done childhood. We've already weathered that storm. It's over. We never have to go back. So, when our kids are going through it, we're their guide, not their sidekick. We can calm down about all the growing-up feelings and let our kids have them without having to re-have them.

"Oh, I'm so sorry. I know that feels terrible. I remember when that happened to me and it hurts so much." We can draw on our memories and empathize with their pain but stop short of solving their problems for them. You never have to have seventh-grade friend drama again. You never have to experience failing a biology test or an algebra teacher being unfair to you. You don't have anyone making fun of you on the bus, and you won't get yelled at by the neighbor . . . probably. Moms, you never have to get your period for the first time again. Dads, your voice will never crack again while answering a question in class. We can guide our kids through all this coming-of-age life stuff without having to experience it. Do not descend into the madness. Draw your child a hot bath, make her a cup of tea, and let her process her adolescence. You're free.

Most of the time, I can remember this. Sometimes there are too many kids screaming at me at once. When all else fails, it's too early to start drinking, and I feel myself slipping, I put myself in time-out. Once my kids were old enough that I didn't worry they'd die if I left them alone for a few minutes, I started locking myself in the bathroom to catch my breath, hiss a prayer, or swear into my elbow. Now that my kids are really old, I lock myself in the bathroom and take a hot bath for thirty minutes. Sometimes we just need a break.

Kids have a way of scanning you up and down, pinpointing your biggest fears and weaknesses, and exploiting the heck out of them. Tiny sociopaths. It's a good thing they're cute. Alex and I have a safe word for one of our kids who pushes all our buttons. When we're on hour thirteen of this kid arguing nonstop all day long and I'm cleaning up dinner and start envisioning hurling the plates at the wall, I call to Alex, "Bojangles!" That's his cue to step in and usher our darling child away. It's always good to have a calm partner. Alex and I take turns, and, thankfully, we haven't encountered a day when we've both needed a rescue at the same time.

Maybe you need a safe word. You're welcome to ours. We happened to pass a Bojangles' restaurant when we were talking about needing a safe word, so as you can see, we're very creative, thoughtful people.

If you don't have anyone to sweep in and save you from yourself, then you can save yourself from yourself. Put yourself in time-out. Time-out for adults is fabulous, and I recommend having a chocolate stash in your time-out location. It's okay to step out and collect yourself. Parents have feelings, too. We aren't androids.

And when you get upset, there's no one to rescue you, you fail to step away in time, and find yourself exploding and words tumbling out of your mouth that you regret, do what your own mom taught you to do. Say you're sorry. We all blow it sometimes. You're not alone. We apologize a lot to our kids because, unfortunately, we mess up a lot.

Don't Bottle: Model Healthy Feelings

In addition to the ways your kids learn to play you like "The Devil Went Down to Georgia," there's also the never-ending deluge of appointments, practices, meetings, and field trips to juggle. The pressure keeps rising, and it can take a toll on your emotions. When I sent my first one off to preschool it felt like a fun experiment, but then I blinked and had three kids in three schools and all the PTO presidents, room moms, principals, and teachers emailed me at the same time, and then my kids brought all the papers home in their backpacks and flung them at me, and I didn't realize I needed admin experience in order to raise humans.

Before I had kids, I thought I was fairly fantastic, no anger issues whatsoever. But the more kids I had and the more snags we've hit, the bigger my anger has grown. It's not the kids' fault. It's just that before I had them, I pretty much took care of what I needed to do for myself all day every day. Once I had kids, I still had all the me-stuff, but I also had a ton of them-stuff, too. I've had to stretch my capacity to be able to handle all the stuff flying at me, but often some of the stuff hits the fan, or my face. The more I tried to shove down all the feelings of inadequacy and frustration I was experiencing, the more they threatened to explode out my mouth, and over the years I've learned to recognize the feelings, be honest about them, and deal with them in a healthy way.

Rather than bottle up all my feelings, I try to model to my kids how to handle them. Talk through how you're feeling, how you could handle it better, and how you're processing it in a healthy way. If you're having a hard day, it's okay to let your kids see you frustrated, sad, mad, or worried, and work through it.

"I'm jealous of a friend and need to recognize that her success takes nothing from me. I'm operating out of a false sense of scarcity. There's plenty for both of us."

"I'm nervous about something at work, and it's making me short-tempered with you, and I'm sorry."

Obviously, we don't want to unload on our kids. They're our children, not our therapists. But if they see me struggling, or heaven forbid, I snap at them in a difficult moment, I want to take the time to unpack a little of what's underneath. When our kids have big feelings, too, we can help them process those feelings, channeling them in positive ways.

Over time, I've noticed that my kids are developing a larger vocabulary for their feelings. They're learning to name them and get to the root of what's causing them. I'm not naturally gifted in this area, but with the help of good therapists and a lot of practice, we're all growing together.

When I feel myself getting and staying angry more and more, and my toolbox of coping strategies isn't cutting it, I know it's time to get away, text my friends, and blow off steam. (Look for the sequel to this book, *Girls' Night Saves Lives*. Namely, the lives of my kids.)

Things We've Learned in Therapy

Our mental health is incredibly important, but so often we neglect it. We're quick to take our kids to the doctor for a physical ailment, but when it comes to the mental health of both our kids and ourselves, we often don't get the help we need. Don't be afraid to make a call.

Over the course of my parenting journey, we've done play therapy, talk therapy, in-home therapy, Trust-Based Relational Intervention (TBRI) therapy, occupational therapy, and speech therapy. If there was a therapy bingo game, we'd totally win. Here are a few of the many things that've helped us regulate our feelings and bodies.

EMDR. For kids and adults who have experienced trauma of some kind, whether it's a difficult move, divorce, a frightening situation, or abuse, EMDR therapy can be incredibly helpful. I honestly would have thought it was hocus-pocus except that a trusted friend told me how it had helped him with childhood trauma, so we tried it for our family and experienced life-changing results. EMDR stands for Eye Movement Desensitization and Reprocessing, and I am not a therapist, so me trying to explain it to you would be like a man trying to explain menstrual cramps. Incoherent and uncomfortable for us both. To find a therapist who is trained in EMDR with children, I asked a therapist friend. If you're interested, ask your doctors for their suggestions and talk to other parents you trust. There's a lot of information online as well, so often when I'm searching for someone specific, I start online but then ask the people I trust locally for their recommendations.

Feelings Chart. Buy a feelings chart, which is basically a poster with cartoon faces all over it displaying various emotions. This helps kids learn language for a whole range of emotions. Instead of just "mad," maybe they're embarrassed or frustrated or scared or nervous. For those of us who struggle to identify our own emotions, it's helpful for us, too. I'm learning to ask myself how I'm feeling, because often I can't tell. You can ask your kid to point to how they're feeling, and as you use the tool, they can learn to point to maybe even several options, because we can feel multiple feelings at the same time. I mean, have you seen the movie *Home*? That Boov learns an important lesson about humans. The sad-mad is real.

Breathing techniques. Regulating our breath helps us calm down. One therapist taught us "balloon breathing." Breathe in and breathe out like you're blowing up a balloon. You can also have your kid breathe in for four counts and breathe out for four counts, if they like counting. Another therapist taught us "circle breathing." Trace your hand in a circle slowly. Each quarter of the circle is a different part of the breath. Start at the top, inhale for four counts. Hold the breath for four counts as your hand circles to the bottom. Then exhale for four counts as your hand comes up and hold the breath for four counts as your hand completes the circle. Repeat. You can increase or decrease the counts depending on what your child, or you, needs.

Exercise. When my kids were younger and they started to pop out of whack, I'd have them do jumping jacks or run laps around the house. Now that they're older, they're in sports or go work out at the gym. Sometimes kids need physical stimulation to regulate themselves. Jumping on a trampoline, hanging upside down on a couch, spinning in a circle, or punching a boxing bag can help. Physical exercise helps reset the brain. Parents need it, too. It's why I do yoga and Zumba. Getting exercise keeps me from crossing into that homicidal category we're all trying to avoid.

Baby burrito. If your kid is small enough, you can wrap him up in a blanket like a burrito, then you and a partner or friend each take one end and gently swing him back and forth. As they get bigger, you can wrap them up and gently roll them on the ground. If they don't calm down, throw guacamole in their face. Just kidding: don't do that. Don't ever waste guacamole.

Meet a physical need. I mentioned this a little in chapter 2. When they were babies and got upset, you figured out if your kids needed their diaper changed, a bottle, or a nap. That doesn't really change when they get older. When your big kid is melting down, meet a physical need. Do they need more sleep because they stayed up too late the night before? Do they have low blood sugar? Help them get a snack. My kids laugh at me, but when they tell me they have a headache, the first thing I say is, "Drink a glass of water." If they're moody and struggling with a relationship or nervous about a test, pour them a cup of tea or share a piece of chocolate. I'm always quick to start talking at them and solve the problem, but sometimes the problem is physical, and meeting a physical need will give them the mental and emotional strength they need to solve the problem on their own.

Flip the script. If you have a kid struggling with negative thinking, help them flip the script. "I can't do that" becomes "I can do hard things." "I can't calm down" becomes "I can calm down." We can do this, too. "I can't drink another cup of coffee" becomes "I can drink one more cup." "I can't wear jammies to the bus stop" becomes "I can wear jammies in public." We have to stay positive, okay?

Drawing. Have them draw pictures of their feelings. One of my kids used to draw the whole family smiling, then a heavy black wall, then me on the other side of the wall. On fire. I was on fire on the other side of a thick wall. I saved this family portrait because that junk is real. Lately, the kid draws all of us together with me in the middle smiling, so things are better. When words fail, drawings are really helpful when your kids are trying to get you to understand how they're feeling.

Give kids choice. When my kids would get upset about having to do something they didn't want to do, I'd give them two choices. I was fine with either choice, and they felt like they had some control and calmed down. For instance, when one of my kids didn't want to go to bed, I'd ask, "Do you want to turn the light off or do you want me to?" Either way, the light goes off, but the kid had a choice in the matter. "Do you want to eat your broccoli before your turkey or after?" "Do you want to brush your teeth before your bath or after your bath?"

Figuring out how I feel about things and taking care of my own mental health does not come easily to me. I would rather shove everything into an internal folder marked "Deal with Later," so I'm thankful that over the years as I've worked hard to meet the needs of my kids, I've learned more how to help myself as well. We're a healthier family because of it.

10 THINGS TO TELL YOUR KIDS AND YOURSELF ABOUT FEELINGS

1. It's okay to feel mad/sad/scared/frustrated/relieved. Your feelings are valid.
2. You can feel multiple emotions at the same time.
3. How does your body feel? Where in your body do you feel this?[9] (If you have a middle schooler, prepare yourself for a joke here.)

---

9 Enneagram coach Lisa Vischer taught me this and it's been a helpful tool for me in learning to connect with my emotions.

4. What do you need right now?
5. I know this is hard right now, but you will feel better. The feelings are important, but they're not forever.
6. You are the boss of your own feelings.
7. How can I help?
8. You're in a safe place.
9. It's okay to cry. (Please tell boys this as often as we tell girls.)
10. What strategy can you use to help process this feeling? (Breathing techniques, spinning in a circle, ideas from the previous section.)

8

People Are Super Awkward, Including You

Lighten Up About Friends

> "A boy's best friend is his mother."
> —*Psycho*

I was one of three girls in my entire kindergarten class, and for giggles, the other two would plan "We Hate Melanie" days. This is probably why to this day I still abhor school spirit days. They'd make a pact not to talk to me all day, so I learned early on to talk to boys, who seemed less complicated. In the spring of that year, we moved from Kentucky to Ohio, and I went from having two girls who sometimes wouldn't talk to me to having a whole class of strangers who told me I talked funny and wondered why I had a country ham hanging in my garage. I ditched the accent as fast as I could and learned to assimilate, thus beginning my career as a chameleon. I couldn't do anything about the weird ham, but I don't care where you're from, once you've tasted Kentucky country ham, you understand the magic.

Developing friendships can be awkward and time-consuming, and everybody approaches it differently. Some of us only need a couple close friends and others need a herd. As a parent, you learn to manage your own friend issues while also keeping an eyeball out for your kids and their budding relationships. Do you remember middle school? I hate to break it to you, but based on my observations, it hasn't gotten any easier. You'd think after all these years the good people at, I don't know, NASA, or maybe the Pope or someone would've solved awkward friend drama for us. But alas, we're still wandering around down here just one step up from wagging tails and sniffing butts. Most of us, anyway.

One of my kids always has a slew of friends. If social butterfly means you need a large quantity of friends, this kid is a social condor. Her wingspan and speed encompass legions of friendships, and she has to interact with someone at all times. I have another kid who needs two friends. Just a couple good friends. Another kid is more like Cinderella, the cartoon version, standing outside all afternoon talking to animals.

Some of us are chameleons like me, trying to fit in wherever we can, and others are like, "This is me. Take it or leave it." I have both kinds of kids in my house, and helping them navigate friendships has been challenging, fun, and at times a little nerve-wracking. Just like when we were kids, at some point there's going to be drama, but we don't have to let it take over our lives.

We need to lighten up about friend drama. I say this, but honestly, I've had several moments of flop sweat over my kids' friends, so we do need to lighten up, but it isn't always easy. When your kids are young, you'll decide their friends based on what moms you want to hang out with. When your kids are older, they decide their friends, and you'll do everything you can to avoid hanging out with their friends' parents. (If you're reading this, parent of my kid's friend, of course I don't mean you. I mean everyone but you, because you're super cool.) In the middle school years, you become the FBI and interrogate your witness before and after every social event while also pretending to be fine and relaxed about the whole thing. I recommend practicing your unfazed face in the mirror before you bust out a bug-eyed Looney Tunes mug when your kid starts a sentence with, "What happened was . . ."

It's fine. We're fine. Everything is fine. We want our kids to find friends, and we probably aren't allowed to bubble wrap them first. Calm down and let's get through this.

Those Joneses

I'm going to talk about our kids' friends, then a bit about our own friends. As our kids get older, their world expands, and this means our world has to expand, too. Thank goodness. The tiny petri dish of the preschool down the street suddenly expands to a huge cosmos of people. Our conversations and the way we approach other families has to broaden to make room for differences. We can't assume everyone is parenting the same way or having the same experiences. We're all different and so are our kids.

Everything widens. Their vocabulary, their options, and the way they see the world. Dinner conversations go from us telling our kids about "spoon," "plate," "yummy green beans," and "Jesus loves you," to trying to figure out how to answer questions like,

"How do we know God's real?" and "What's sex? And have you and Daddy ever done it?"

We're not the only voices in their lives anymore. Now they have friends. The wheels on the bus go round and round, and the kids on the bus try to share what they've heard, and it's all rather confusing. So, we unravel it over chicken nuggets.

When your kids have friends, at some point they're going to compare you to their friends' parents, and you will be found wanting, because as we all know, everyone else's parents are better, cooler, and richer than us. When we were growing up, people thought they had to keep up with the Joneses, but these days the bar is even higher. My kids think we have to keep up with the Kardashians, too.

As a young kid, I wore a lot of hand-me-downs from my super-cool neighbors down the street, and if we ran through a drive-thru, my mom didn't let us get drinks, because "we have drinks at home." We always had plenty, but I grew up knowing the value of money and having a sense of frugality that's served me well as the society around me has developed a case of the munchies.

You know what I mean? We '80s kids grew up drinking out of the hose and eating Velveeta, and now we order five-dollar coffees and get mad if the barista uses the wrong kind of nut milk. Everything has swelled out of proportion. We run around putting on airs, and maybe we need to hearken back to our days of fishing hand-me-downs out of the bag the neighbor dropped off.

My kids come home from school talking about what their friends have and how things are working in other people's homes, and I tell them it's my job to give them a sweet reality check, because both the lenience and opulence are not normal. Your kids will tell you that EVERYONE has the new iPhone,

CALM THE H*CK DOWN

EVERYONE is vaping, EVERYONE went to the Taylor Swift concert, or EVERYONE gets fourteen hours of screen time a day. Whatever our kids want, they'll try to use the power of peer pressure on us, because they think if we think everyone else is doing it, then we'll let them do it, too. What they don't know is we've already been hardened by years of withstanding our own peer pressure and their attempts to sway us are meaningless. And if you do ever feel swayed by what all the other parents are allowing, I promise you we're not. We're super stodgy, too, so let's all agree not to compete with each other.

Even if we could keep up with the Joneses, maybe we don't have to. Find friends who share your values, and if you're like me and love a good bag of hand-me-downs, buddy up to some people with kids a year or two older.

Helping Your Kids Develop Healthy Friendships

Remember the first time you invited someone over for a play date and your kid started raking Legos into their shirt so the interloper couldn't play with them? You were embarrassed and spent the next hour saying, "Now, honey, we need to share," in a singsongy voice, wondering what happened to your adorable child. Human nature is a beast, and if left to our own devices, we will hoard food, steal toys, and push people around to get what we want. I mean, have you seen a grocery store in the South when we're expecting a half inch of snow? We have to teach our spawn some civility or society will collapse, and we'll end up bludgeoning each other in the bread aisle.

You start with basic etiquette, and you build on it. When your children have friends over to play, show them how to be good hosts, how to offer snacks and drinks, how to share and take turns, and how to be hospitable. Kids can be clueless and run off, and you find their friend wandering around the kitchen, alone in a stranger's house. Your kid might get a snack for themselves and eat it in front of their friend silently. Is this a power move? Are they establishing themselves as the alpha dog, or are they just too oblivious to realize they should offer their friend a snack, too?

When it comes to having friends over, lighten up about having the fun house. I hear people all the time say they want to have the fun house so everyone will hang out there. People justify buying huge homes, installing ginormous TVs, and digging pools in their backyards in the quest to be the fun house. Maybe your house isn't that fun. It's okay. Look for opportunities to let your kid invite friends to go do things, whether it's a movie or dinner or a trip to the zoo. One time I loaded up our van with middle schoolers and took them to sort toys for foster kids. Service projects are not historically fun. But they had a good time anyway and got to help others. (And if you do have a fun house, please invite us over.)

As your kids approach that in-between age of being kind of older but still little, you start to wonder when it's okay to foist them at a responsible adult and back away slowly. Your entire life becomes a song from the Clash, "Should I Stay or Should I Go." I sat through reptile-themed birthday parties and pool dates wondering if I should be there or if the other parent was wishing I'd leave so she could quit making small talk with me. The general rule of thumb for play dates and parties is once the kids are in elementary school and you know the parents well enough to feel confident in their ability to keep your kid alive and safe, you can drop off and don't have to stay. I'm declaring this here, so now you can cite a book when questioned, 'cos everything in books must be true. When in doubt if it's a drop-off scenario, just ask ahead of time.

As our kids enter middle school and beyond, our own friendships become an underground spy network sharing intel and keeping tabs on everyone. Develop your network. Chat up other moms and dads at events and practices so that when you hear things, you can contact the network and check your sources. It takes a village, for sure.

I'd describe my parenting style here in the teen years as "relaxed inquisitioner." I have a million questions about every little thing, but if my kids are answering them openly or willing to help me find the answers, then I'm fairly trusting. If they start to hedge, I get curious about what they're hiding. When they get home, I have a million more questions, but if it's a give and take, and I feel like they're telling me stuff, even if it's stuff I wish I could un-know and possibly gouge my eyes out over, I feel good about it. Pretty much "keep them talking" is the name of the game. The more open the conversations we have with our kids, the more we can lighten up and stop worrying over everything.

When your kid tells you things the other kids are doing, don't act shocked. Ask follow-up questions and get your kid's perspective before you go into lecture mode. Your kid might already be doing the right thing and is trusting you with this insider scoop. This is an opportunity to affirm your kid's good instincts.

Over and over, after big conversations, I hear myself saying, "I'm so glad you told me. Thanks so much for trusting me with this." I want to hear the things, and I'd rather them learn by processing these things with me than by my doling out punishments to terrify them into submission. Don't get me wrong, those are fine, too. "Your phone is now mine for a while. Give me my phone." Such a great deterrent.

If your kid gets invited somewhere and you don't know the parents, ask for their number and make a phone call. Don't let your kid talk you into thinking this is weird or you're the only clingy parent. I'm doing it, too, and other parents call me all the time.

"Who all's going?" "Let me call her mom and make sure she's okay with it." "Where will you be?" "Text me if you leave there and go somewhere else." I parent with the assumption that I can trust my kids unless they prove otherwise. I ask all the questions, contact parents as needed, gather all the facts, and then say yes and let them go, and as long as they're faithful to keep me informed and do what they say they'll do and be where they say they'll be, then we're good. If they step out of line, it's time to rein in the leash a bit.

Yes, there is a downside to all the cell phones, but the glorious upside is that you can always get hold of your kid, and it works like a pocket LoJack. We can track exactly where our kids are and call them to come home or show up unexpectedly to crash the party any time we want.

During these years, whoever your kid is hanging out with will determine the path they're on and the choices they make. So, it's important to keep tabs on who they're spending time with. I disagree with "social engineering" and manipulating your kid's friend group, but I think we need to be aware if someone is being mean or destructive and put some limits in place. If you see your child's behavior start to change, do a little digging to figure out what could be causing the change, whether they're imitating their

favorite YouTube channel or spending too much time with someone whose values are really different than your family's. If you feel
like your kid is following a group down the wrong path, it's okay
to have them take a break. You're not judging the friends. You're
judging your kid's behavior and helping them get back on track.

Resist the urge to demonize another kid. As a society, we've
sort of run out of grace for each other's children. We call the cops
or the school before we have a conversation. We assume the other
parent is raising a monster who must be stopped, so we do our
part and send for Van Helsing. Let's just calm down.

Mean Kids

Not a week goes by when I don't see a Facebook conversation
about protecting our kids from mean kids, but what about when
your kid is the mean kid? Kids can be mean and haul off and
say something thoughtless or cruel. We adults do it all the time
and supposedly we benefit from impulse control and years of
experience. So, of course, our darlings are going to flap their lips
in the wrong direction from time to time. My kids have been both
on the giving and receiving ends of meanness, and probably most
kids can relate. I know I can.

There's a difference between bullying and meanness, and we
need to determine which situations require adult intervention
and which don't. One of my kids was on the receiving end of a
widescale hate campaign, and the school got involved. This was
bullying, and we adults had to step in. But most of the other slights
and dings that happen during a school day help kids learn relational boundaries and coping skills. When my kids claim they're

being bullied because someone ignored them on the playground, my husband likes to remind them how he spent the better part of a school year stuffed in a locker. There's a difference.

Coach from the Sidelines and Do Not Get on the Field

When your kids get older and start experiencing friend drama beyond the basics of sharing toys and biting, do your best to stay out of their relationships and let them handle things on their own. Seriously. Stand down. Many times, parents getting involved in their older kids' friendships cause more problems than they solve. (I'm not talking about the bullying, the abuse, the crime, the serious, serious stuff. You know what I mean. There's a difference between "Richard said he didn't like my shirt" and "Richard threatened me with a tire iron in the parking lot.")

Think of it like coaching. We need to coach our kids and model healthy relationships to them. I have one million conversations with my kids about how to treat people, how not to gossip, and how to show kindness. I call them out when they're in the wrong. We dissect every situation and look for the ways they screwed up and the ways other people treated them. I offer advice. We run plays, go over scripts, and ask questions.

"Do this not that." "He reacted this way because you did this." "You can't control his behavior, but you can control yours." "I get that she hurt you and I'm sorry and that's wrong. Is there a small piece of this that you can own and make amends for?" "How could you have handled this differently?" "When you said this, what do you think she heard? Why might that have offended her?"

Our job as parents is to teach our kids how to treat people and how to be treated. How to recognize toxic behavior. How to get out of a relationship if it's toxic and learn to protect themselves. How to stick up for themselves and for others. How to ask for help. How to ask for forgiveness when they've screwed up. How to make it right. Teach your kids how to apologize when they mess up. Role-play apologizing in person. Help them write apology notes. Model apologizing to them when you're the one who screwed up and you need to ask them for forgiveness.

But unless it's a safety issue, that's where our job ends. We can teach our kids how to navigate friendships without actually fighting their battles for them or throwing down with other parents. Our kids have to learn how to maintain friendships themselves. We coach from the sidelines, but we don't get on the field. That's where our kids are, and it's up to them to play the game.

I've cringed so hard listening to my kids talk about what they did or what someone said. And I think back to my own cringe-worthy behavior when I was their age. I'm so glad my mom didn't show up to school every time someone was mean to me, but I'm also glad I could talk to her about it and get her advice. Sometimes I wished I'd actually taken more of it.

They have to learn some lessons the hard way. We can teach our kids not to gossip over and over, but until they do it, get called out for it, and lose a friend, they won't always listen. Talk to your kids about keeping their friends' confidences and not gossiping. Teach them that people who talk trash about others will turn around and do it to them. Show them how to be careful who they trust and call them out if they're the ones who betray a friend.

It's devastating to watch them hurt. But it's important, too.

Recently my kid was having friend troubles, asked for forgiveness about something, had more friend troubles, and felt betrayed. Through it all, I listened and consoled and hugged and offered advice. A few days later the two of them were arm in arm. All better. They did it. They made it through, hugged it out, and developed key relationship strategies in the process. If I had involved myself directly, calling the other mom or inserting myself into the fight, the fallout would've been bigger, and they might never have recovered. For kids, things are over in a flash. For parents, we hold grudges for people who hurt our kids. Don't activate the mama bear unless you're prepared to get mauled.

Some kids are pretty even-keeled, but others are characters in their own personal soap opera. And you might be the most undramatic person in the world and have a kid who is constantly in the thick of it. Stay the course, parent. Remain as neutral as possible, console and advise as needed, and let them walk through their own tunnel of chaos. It will get better once their brains grow up and they develop a little more steadiness and logical reasoning. I mean, look how awesome we all are now. Okay, bad example.

Smartphones Will Systematically Hunt and Kill Us All

To read my Facebook feed, smartphones are literally hunting and killing our children, picking them off one by one. Okay, I know there's inherent danger in giving our babies access to the whole internet at the touch of a finger, absolutely, but let's calm down before we drive ourselves bananaballs. When it comes to presenting our kids with this all-access pass, it doesn't have to be all or nothing. You can do a soft launch and roll out apps at whatever pace feels right, and you can rein back in when needed. Don't just plop an iPhone in your kid's hand with all the bells and whistles. Take it one app at a time.

Smartphones are both a blessing and a curse when it comes to friend dynamics. When I was a teen, you left the drama at school, for the most part. When you got home, the only access you had to the outside world was one home phone line, and only then if your mom wasn't already using it to order something out of the JCPenney catalogue. You'd wait your turn, then when you finally could use the phone, you'd stand in the kitchen in front of your sibling, mom, and the neighborhood boys who were over to play Legos with your brother. If you were very lucky, maybe you had your own phone extension in your room, but even then, your mom would pick up every now and then and ask how much longer you were going to be because she needed to call your dad at work, and you could only call one friend at a time and only if they had access to their home phones. So, the amount of drama you could create was contingent on very limited phone access. When I got three-way calling on my Swatch phone, I thought I'd die with happiness. I'd ask my friends if they wanted to have a three-way, and everyone seemed very excited about it until the movie *Threesome* came out and blew our minds. I had to leave the room, I was so kerfloofy and I never looked at my Swatch phone the same.

These days everyone has their own phone, and the second they get on the bus after school, they're texting. And they aren't just texting one person. They're group texting. Your kid might have five different group chats going on at once, and if someone could figure out how to harness the energy being generated from millions of thumbs typing into these phones in various group chats across the country, we could say good-bye to fossil fuels, save the fossils entirely, and probably stop global warming. I don't know science.

The words are flying, and anyone can screenshot any part of it and take it out of context. And there's no break. So the drama grows and expands, and pretty soon your kid is upset and you don't know why because you thought they were just doing homework by themselves in their room, but they were actually hanging out talking crap with fourteen other people, and it got out of hand and everyone's mad at everyone.

Here's the good news. As parents, we can take the phone away. Heck, we even have the technology to lock the whole phone or specific apps remotely.

"Here, honey, you can listen to music, but we turned off your friends for a while. They'll be waiting for you at school tomorrow."

Does my kid get mad when I do this? Briefly. We actually take great pleasure in turning off their phone remotely, then listening to them scream in frustration as they realize we've locked them out.

My husband flicks a switch on his phone, then says, "Wait for it . . . three . . . two . . . one . . ." And from across the house we hear, "NOOOOOO!" Since we're heartless bastards, we giggle sadistically.

But the handful of times we've had to do this, the kid starts mad and ends grateful. Just like our parents wouldn't let us use the home phone, we can take away our kids' cell phones and not only when they're in trouble. We get to rescue them from themselves.

I know there's a movement to wait to give kids smartphones until eighth grade,[10] and I think that's great if that works for you. We did things a little differently, in some ways being more lenient and in other ways being stricter. We gave our kids smartphones after elementary school, before they were heading into sixth grade, and the school makes all the kids keep them in their lockers during the day. My kids have phones, but they still don't have internet access. We approve or deny apps, they can earn apps and screen time, and we can get hold of them when they're out with friends. We can even track their location using the Life360 app and watch them move around the neighborhood like we're freaking spies on stakeout in a van.

When we started, they had music and could take photos, but they had no social media, so what happened on their phones stayed on their phones. We didn't have a set time when we'd let them have social media, but we wanted to delay it until they'd developed a bit of impulse control, and when we finally did acquiesce, we started with one app at a time.

I know how detrimental social media can be in my own life, and I want to protect my kids from that as long as possible and give them time to develop critical thinking and the ability to think better of a post and delete it before hitting Publish or Share. Each kid is different. Know your child and go slowly. It isn't all or nothing. It's baby steps.

Last year one of my kids came up to us and gave us a big hug. We looked at each other quizzically and then they shocked us with, "Thank you for not letting me have social media." Don't be too excited, because my kids spend the majority of their time

---

10 Wait Until 8th Pledge, *Wait Until 8th*. https://www.waituntil8th.org/.

being the opposite of thankful about this decision, but we soaked up that one moment where the teen veil lifted and they realized, if briefly, that we were protecting them from not only internet weirdos but also themselves. Not a day goes by that I don't thank God we didn't have social media when I was in junior high or there'd be video proof of me naïvely crooning "I Touch Myself." I do wish we'd had the internet, because easy access to song lyrics might've prevented some embarrassing moments.

When we finally let Ana get her first social media app, Alex gave her a rule for posting: no swears, slurs, or sexiness. The internet is forever.

Alex: We're always watching.
Ana: Stalker much?
Alex: No, parent much.

Alex monitors all the tech in the house, and one way he's been able to lighten up is by managing everything at the router level using Circle with Disney. Rather than having to load and manage protective software on each child's computer or phone, he manages every connected device on our home wifi network at the router level, including downtime and content restrictions. He can also set time limits, restrict apps and content, and schedule downtime remotely from his own phone using the Screen Time settings on the iPhone. Even with these limits, our kids turn in their phones to us at 9:00 p.m., because they just don't need screens by their little heads beckoning to them all night long. If our kids want new apps or songs, they have to request permission, and he gets a notice on his phone that our kid wants something. He reviews it, then approves or disapproves the request through iPhone Family

Sharing. Okay, maybe we are stalkers, but I feel good about it. (There are lots of alternatives to Circle and the iPhone features, but these are the ones we use. By the time your kid has a phone, we might be mind-melding like Spock. I can't know these things.)

When it comes to social media, texting, and smartphones, you know your kids better than anyone. Set the boundaries your unique child needs and calm down about what everyone else is doing.

So that's enough about our kids' friends. Now what about ours?

Your Friends

Training our kids to develop healthy relationships is a huge part of parenting, so they need to see us have healthy relationships, cultivate new friends, maintain old friends, and prioritize connections. Also, parenting in a vacuum can feel really lonely. Friends help me feel like we're going to survive the pace and pressure of these parenting years. Friends calm each other down.

My kids regularly see me head out on a Friday night to meet my friends for dinner, or come home to find a large tub of popcorn from the movie I saw with a friend while they were in school. They see me make dinner for friends when they have a sick kid, and my friends come to our rescue when we're the ones in need. I want my kids to see me plugged into our community and know we're surrounded by healthy relationships and that they are safe and loved. I also want them to know these relationships don't just happen. We have to work on them. Probably the question I get asked most by parents is, "How do we find and develop friendships?"

My thoughts on finding friends during the early-childhood

years could fill a whole book, which they do, called *Women Are Scary: The Totally Awkward Adventure of Finding Mom Friends.*[11] My biggest advice about finding friends during this stage is to look close to home. Whether it's the park near your house, your neighborhood community pool, or the laundry room in your apartment building, look for friends with kids the same age and strike up awkward conversations with them until something sticks. Whether you're standing in line to check your kid into the child care at your gym or place of worship, yelling on the sideline at a soccer game, or in the observation room at dance class, find people doing the same things you're doing in the same places you already are. If you're commuting across town an hour to meet a friend, it's going to be hard to maintain, and she certainly can't run over with saltines and bananas when your kid has the barfs.

Look for friends already in your kinesphere and then prioritize spending time with them. I can spend all day in my minivan schlepping kids around, pull into my driveway, close the garage door behind me, and never interact with my neighbors if I don't make it a priority. I know you're busy. Make a plan, make a date, and have a cup of coffee. When our kids are small, friends help us feel normal and increase our capacity to handle both the exhaustion and utter mundanity of keeping little ones alive.

Mothers still in the childbearing stage, a note: some people don't want to hear about your cervix or inverted nipples. There are two kinds of parents in the world: those who embrace—dare I say, enjoy—the body oddities that come with the job and those who handle them but prefer not to think about them, much less discuss them in a group. This far into the book, you know which

---

11 Melanie Dale, *Women Are Scary* (Grand Rapids, MI: Zondervan, 2015).

one I am. But those of us oversharers must learn the hard reality that not everyone wants to hear about our mucous plugs and horizontally spreading side-pubes. (You start with a standard triangle, but then you get pregnant and it morphs into more of a rectangle, or even a pentagon. Your babymaker looks like it's preparing to host the Joint Chiefs of Staff.)

But some people don't want to hear about it. Their loss, I say. I like gross body stuff at all ages and stages. If your kid's diaper falls off at the top of the slide in the Chick-fil-A playland and he proceeds to slide all the way down wearing nothing but banana-colored diarrhea and a smile, I want all the details. If you keep finding crunchy socks in your teen son's hamper and your washing machine isn't fixing it, let's figure this out together. Tell me about your irritable bowel. Recommend the oil for the hemorrhoid. I am ready to listen. Maybe not ready to apply the oil, but ready to hear you on the subject.

As our kids grow out of the baby and toddler stages, we need to respect their privacy, so before we go spewing intimate details, make sure it's a trusted friend and not a whole dinner party, and definitely don't put it on the internet, says the author blogger. (In my defense, now that my kids are older, I always get their permission before sharing on the internet. Which is why my Instagram feed looks like I don't have a son anymore. Once in a while I beg him to let me post a proof-of-life photo.) As for our own stuff, share what you like, but if you notice the eyes of the people around you darting away like trapped animals, let your friend go back to her rabbit hutch and find someone else as gross as you.

Really, the most important thing that changes from preschool play dates to elementary school is the need for decent carpooling options. I used to spend all my time chatting up other moms at parks while our daughters, strangers mere minutes ago, ran off arm in arm to conquer the corkscrew slide. But then in elementary school my kids started choosing their own friends. I would drop them off at a friend's house, or they'd simply run out the door into the cul-de-sac where they'd meet up with their pack and roam our street on bikes. (I've seen enough shows to know they were probably encountering creepy clowns, running from the Fratellis, or rescuing a friend from the Upside Down.) But while they developed more freedom of choice with their relationships, their schedules got a little tighter.

We'll talk about activities in chapter 10, but let's talk about the need to buddy up with decent carpool friends right here. My son started swimming on the year-round team, with practices five times a week all the way on the other side of town. After one season of that, I knew I needed to make some swim friends.

I like all the parents in our carpool immensely, but even if I didn't, we aren't there to hang out. No, each afternoon we convene at the nearby convenience store parking lot simply to chuck sweaty boys, flippers, and goggles into one of our vans. One friend is in charge of scheduling, and we all drive a few times a month, and you'd better own a van big enough to haul a whole lot of boys. I feel like I won the lottery with the swimming thing because when I have six boys in my van after a two-hour practice, I just smell chlorine. It's heavenly, and I'll take it over the post-soccer or -lacrosse practice stenches of my girls any day.

These boys don't all have that much in common, and they span three grade levels, but every day they spend the afternoon together, and I love listening to their conversations because the one rule of carpool is that the driver doesn't really exist and definitely can't hear. I've heard who likes whom, what drama is happening at school, and several dirty jokes they don't know that I know they know. I try to do my part and introduce them to decent music, so I pump Aerosmith, Guns N' Roses, and Queen through my minivan's speakers. But I skip "Fat Bottomed Girls" because that feels disrespectful, and I don't want to be responsible for a vanload of young men running around talking inappropriately of rumps, even if we are living in a post–J. Lo world of backside liberation.

The parenting years can produce more friends of convenience than kindred spirits, but hang out long enough and you may find a soul mate in there, too. I have a handful of besties who meet regularly for girls' night, and if I go too long without seeing them, I get a little jittery. The pressure of parenting builds up over time, and hanging out with other parents who understand and like me in spite of myself releases the steam. My husband has his friends, too, and they get together for poker or bourbon around a firepit. No matter how busy you get with your kids' schedules at this age, find time to develop and maintain your own friends, too. If your kids are in school, do lunch. Actually, I have to wrap up this paragraph now because I'm meeting a couple people for a day beer before the kids come home.

10 THINGS TO TALK ABOUT BESIDES YOUR KIDS

When we do finally get to hang out with our friends, sometimes it's hard thinking of things to talk about besides parenting. But surely there's other stuff going on besides who's getting braces and which kid keeps waking up in the middle of the night. What else can we talk about? Here are some ideas:

1. What are you working on?
2. What are you learning?
3. What are you watching?
4. What are you reading?
5. What do you do for yourself to stay calm?
6. Tell a funny story.
7. Talk about the news.
8. What's something you wish you knew when you were younger?
9. If you could travel anywhere, where would you go?
10. Dream about what you'll do when you're gloriously empty-nesting.

What Happens in the Backpack Stays in the Backpack

Lighten Up About School

"Well, I gotta look on the bright side. Maybe
I can still get kicked out of school."
—*Buffy the Vampire Slayer*

The skin on my hands is rough and raw. I blame backpacks, because every time I touch my kids' backpacks, I feel the need to scour my fingers to the bone and sanitize underneath my fingernails. I try to avoid the backpacks as much as possible, making my children hand me papers of importance and pack and unpack their own stuff, but inevitably I end up going in for something. It's a dumpster dive like no other.

The backpacks develop strata over the school year. The top layer consists of loose-leaf paper, notes from friends, and crumpled permission slips I was supposed to sign two weeks ago. The middle layer is for pencils, chewed up erasers, and glue sticks that have lost their caps. The bottom layer is the one to really avoid, for it is where snacks go to die in a crumbled mess that slowly decays throughout the year, becoming sentient and whispering oddly specific schoolyard taunts. By May, it slowly digests library books like the Sarlacc from the planet Tatooine. When the final notices from the librarian start arriving the second week of May, go ahead and pay the fee, because those books are long gone. It's a small price to pay to appease the creature living on your child's back.

It's fitting that today of all days I sat down to work on the chapter about school, as I just signed my kids' report cards last night. My three kids have three very different ways of presenting me with their report cards.

Distraction and Nonchalance

"It's fine, Mom, see look over here and see this and this and it's cool it's great this is even better than what you were hoping for don't worry about it everything's under control." (*Waves hands, rubs my back, gesticulates and smiles reassuringly.*)

Sullenness and Tears

"Here. It's not my fault. I hate all my teachers I am a total victim it's them and not me never ever doing homework I thought for sure I'd get good grades if I just watched more TV." (*Sobs uncontrollably.*)

Total Oblivion

"What? We got report cards? What's a grade? Do I have grades? Are they good? What does 'needs improvement' mean? Is this even my report card? What's my name again?" (*Cultivates innocent face.*)

I was planning on raising supernerds who would study too much, join marching band, and watch documentaries for fun, but my kids decided to go another way. So this is a fantastic time for me to remind myself to lighten the heck up about school.

Before we lighten up about the actual school days, we have to lighten up about the school itself. Part of parenting is teaching our kids stuff, and most of us reading this book have some choice in how we do that. I chose my kids' preschool because it was literally the closest one to my house and it ended up being awesome. We freak ourselves out about school. And I get it: school's a big issue. If you have choice in this area, then that's a privilege so take a sec to appreciate that you even get to have this stress in your life. Not everyone has a choice, because of location, finances, schedules, or temperament.

I know quite a few people who are able to homeschool. If you homeschool, that's great for you. If I homeschooled, I'd end up in the paper: "Georgia Mother Tosses Kids to Lions in Fit of Rage at Zoo Atlanta during Homeschool Field Trip." I don't have anything to say about it except that I'm cheering you on.

My husband went to private school and he turned out pretty fabulous. As a bonus, he looks adorable in all his old school pictures wearing his preppy little uniform, as opposed to how I dressed myself for picture day. I look like I hired Carmen Miranda to be my stylist. During a brief period in which Ana's visa wouldn't allow her to attend public school, we tried to get her in private school, but the administrators wouldn't let her in and assured me, "But we did pray about it." I was like, "You mean God said no?" Don't tell my daughter that God said no about her attending school or she'll drop out tomorrow with pleasure.

I went to public school and that's where we decided to send our kiddos. But feel free to do whatever, because I don't know your life. Everyone worries about whether or not we're making the right choices for our kids. First, you worry about what kind of education you want them to have, then it's which teachers, what curriculum, which classes, what test prep . . . the list goes on. In my house, we're trying to set the bar fairly low and just go for kids who can hold down jobs and pay rent, so they don't keep living with us indefinitely. So, if that's the goal, then we can relax a bit about the individual grades and test scores. (If you're determined your kids will go to Harvard, you should probably read my next book in the series, *Harder Faster Longer: Under No Circumstances Should You Lighten Up Ever*. And good luck and may all your dreams come true.)

You Can Say No to Stuff

Anyway, send your kids wherever you want or have to send them, say a prayer, and shove them out the door into the world. It'll be great. The first thing that'll happen is you'll get punched in the face. Not literally punched in the face. Most schools aren't like a 1980s after-school special about bullying. No, you will be punched by aggressive volunteerism. After registering your child for school, they know your name, where you live, and how to reach you, and you're a goner. Parent involvement at school is just . . . so involved. Repeat after me: no. You can say no, over and over.

When my kids first started school, I got overly excited and signed up for everything. They had a big parent fair in the cafeteria, and I walked from table to table, writing down my email and signing up to sell ice cream, volunteer in the classroom, and receive more information about scouts and the little after-school Christian club and cultural arts and juggling. I thought it all sounded awesome. And then the following week the emails started coming in and my inbox was inundated. I realized I'd made a horrible miscalculation. School could not be my full-time job. I already had one. I started deleting and unsubscribing and apologizing as I backstepped my way out of commitment after commitment. Rookie mistake.

The school years are a marathon, not a sprint. You're going to be there for a while, so take a deep breath, put on your comfiest yoga pants, and figure out what you can handle. Start small. Don't sign up for room mom right out of the gate, unless you're like, "This is what I've been training for," in which case, thank you for your service. Many of us sign up for things because we feel guilty and they need someone. But everything will get done, and if it doesn't, well, we probably didn't need it anyway. The teachers are doing the heavy lifting of teaching, and we just need to provide the occasional assist.

You don't have to go to every school party and holiday lunch. You can if you want to, but your kid will survive if you can't. I don't attend everything, but when I am there, I try to make a point to invite my child's friends to sit with us if their parents can't be there. Maybe their parent couldn't get off work this time. I ask the kid, "What does your mom do?" And then I gush. "Oh my gosh, that's amazing! She sounds so cool. That's such an important job!" If I know the parent, I take a photo of her kid and text it to her, letting her know we had a great time.

My friends do that for me. When I'm writing or speaking

somewhere and can't chaperone the field trip or attend the class party, my friends send me photos of my kid having a great time, and I try to do that for other parents when I'm there and they aren't. We don't all have to show up all the time. We can pinch hit for each other and make sure all the kids feel loved and supported.

I hate class parties. I feel awkward and don't know what to do with a bunch of kids running around with glue and glitter. One time I showed up and my daughter asked, "What are you doing here? Please leave now." Did she sense my discomfort or was my presence in her classroom cramping her first-grade style? Since then she's invited me to several and I've awkwardly skulked in the back of the class not sure what to do with my hands.

We stand around gaping at our kids while they smear frosting on cookies and talk to their friends, and sometimes there are just too many of us and we're like creepers. Why do a bunch of third-graders need paparazzi snapping iPhone photos of their every move? Back in my day, only the room moms showed up for parties, with their Jell-O Jigglers and holiday cookies. We ate a bunch of sugar, they passed out treat bags, and then we got on with our lives without the parental peanut gallery staring us down uploading everything to Instagram. If you can't make a party or holiday lunch, really, it's okay. And if you can, but you think it's weird, too, I won't tell.

Every fall there's a signup sheet at Meet the Teacher Night where you can sign up to be the room mom. I've been dodging this for like a decade now and I don't see it changing. I will never be your room mom. Ever.

I'm so grateful for the women who do sign up to be room moms. (Are there room dads? If there is a room dad, I'm sure he's getting his own reality show and they're writing anthems about him because when a dad shows up and does something incredible like parenting his own kid, they have viral Buzzfeed articles about it. A dad did his daughter's ponytail! A dad! All by himself!)

As a deadbeat non-room mom, I do try to sign up for things when they ask for help. We don't all have to lead, but we all can pitch in sometimes. Pro tip: when signing up to send in supplies with your kids, choose lightweight items or you're stuck hand delivering them yourself. Think paper goods or snack foods, rather than drinks or fruit trays. Stick with items small enough to fit in your kid's backpack. When signup lists go out, check your email quickly to get your first choice, or you may be stuck with the dreaded cupcake or craft project with a "see this Pinterest link" attached, at which point your only option is to transfer schools or let your kid drop out.

As for school spirit days, they can suck it. When I was a kid, I remember we had pajama day, a hat day, and a team day where we all wore Cleveland Browns jerseys and enjoyed a day of dauntless love for Bernie Kosar. Just like everything else in this world, spirit days have swelled in size and frequency. We don't just have spirit days. There are spirit weeks. That's weeks, plural. And if you have multiple kids in multiple schools, you're going to need a chart.

Thankfully, my son couldn't care less. I ask him if he wants to do jammie day and he looks at me like I've lost my mind. My youngest loves spirit days, but she's very involved in the planning and it's up to her to remember when they are. I help with the execution of her vision.

I refuse to participate in Red Ribbon Week until someone produces a study that directly links school spirit days to a decrease in drug use. No one is at a frat party at college going, "Nope, I'm gonna skip the weed because when I was eight, I wore tie-dye on Thursday to keep kids off drugs."

If you ask any parent, May is the very worst month of the year. You hate your kids, school, and the entire institution of parenting, and you wonder what you ever did to deserve this much stress. Last week my middle schooler asked if I'd received an email from school. Which one? I get thirty a day, per school, per class. No matter how many I delete without opening, they keep popping up in my inbox, like little copulating reminders of my ineptitude. If you haven't learned to say no throughout the rest of the school year, definitely sac up by May, or you will not survive it.

Advocating for Your Kids When You're Still Kinda Scared of the Principal's Office

I got called into the principal's office. Again. As a people-pleasing student who tried hard to get on every teacher's good side, I die inside every time a teacher or principal needs to talk to me about one of my kids.

It happens quite often. And even though I've been doing this for a whole lot of years, my insides still quake when I see that familiar email pop up in my inbox or Caller ID on my phone. Some of my kids are just different than I am and have different needs, struggles, and gifts. And so, I keep getting called to the principal's office.

I actually see these meetings and conversations as incredible opportunities. My kids go to a school where the staff cares about them and wants them to succeed. And they want to partner with me. I could not be more grateful. The parent-teacher relationship is a standard Jerry Maguire situation: "Help me help you." They're helping our kids and we help them help our kids.

So, the number one piece of advice I have to lighten up when it comes to partnering with the school is to recognize that you're on the same team. If defensiveness creeps up and you want to say, "Not my kid!" remember that you're on the same team and everyone wants what's best for your kid. Teachers have a unique perspective that we don't have. They see our kids in a classroom setting. They see how they interact with their peers when we aren't looking. They see what happens when our kid gets frustrated, and they can tell when our kid doesn't understand something.

When it comes to simple phone calls or one-on-one meetings with a teacher, I just try to have a casual conversation. It's usually an exchange of information. "How can I help your child?" "Do you have any suggestions for what would help?" If it's a more formal meeting like an IEP (Individualized Education Program) meeting, I keep a binder with any documents I have from therapists and doctors, as well as some loose-leaf paper for taking notes. I try to write down everyone's name and role at that conference table so I can keep track of who's helping my child.

There have been a few times when I've recorded the meeting, because you have the right to do that. I want to be able to go back and listen to what people said if I didn't understand it or can't remember it. In the academic world, they use acronyms and test names and things the average parent has never heard of, and it's helpful to have a record to go back to. And these meetings can feel intimidating when you walk into a room with five or seven educators. They may be perfectly wonderful, but just being the newcomer in the room can feel overwhelming.

Now, if you're in a situation where everyone is not perfectly wonderful, and your child is not getting the services they need, then find a special education advocate or lawyer, read up on your rights under IDEA (Individuals with Disabilities Education Act), and go get 'em, fierce warrior. Don't be afraid to speak up, ask questions, and insist on what your kid needs. Collect your data, study hard, take notes, and show up prepared. You are the expert on your kid.

This stuff is not light. It's hard and sometimes scary watching our kids struggle and need help. I've found that the more information I have, the more qualified people I have on my team, the more I can lighten up and advocate for my kids. I've learned to lighten up about labels. I used to be scared of labels or anyone pigeonholing my kid into a . . . hole of a pigeon, but now I find that labels and categories can be helpful for getting kids the services they need to thrive and grow. I've come to look forward to these meetings for the information they provide. But I also know that after a big meeting at the school, I'm going to feel drained and overexposed, so I try to take it easy afterward. Treat yourself to a lunch out, order pizza for dinner, plan to take a hot bath, or grab coffee with a trusted friend. (And right here is why you can pry the Oxford comma from my cold, dead hand. Without it, I'd be telling you to take a hot bath with a trusted friend. Or maybe that's what you're planning to do. You know what? That's up to you, but I'm gonna leave that comma there.)

Homework Is Torture for Parents

In my world, homework is a vortex of despair constantly trying to suck me in. It's daily, relentless, and a fact of life for the foreseeable future. I'm constantly on the prowl for ways to lighten up about this heavy albatross. I keep reminding myself that I am not the one in school. My kids are. Really, even if I wanted to help, all my kids' homework stuff is online, and I have no idea what their passwords are or how to make the Google work. I feel relief when I see them bring an actual worksheet home. One thing that helps me lighten up is that I literally can't help them. They changed math. Math isn't even math anymore.

Probably the number one piece of parenting advice I can give is to find the carrot to dangle in front of your kid and dangle it hard. Every kid is motivated differently, so it may take a bit to figure out what little Crowley needs to do his chores, homework, or piano practice. Whether it's positive affirmation, negative consequences, or a combination, pay attention to what drives your kid and milk the heck out of it to get what you want and what they need. One of my kids needs to do homework right after school before I let them have screen time and another needs a break to get the wiggles out first. I parent each kid individually. Dangle different carrots for different kids.

Reading is a huge part of homeworking, and if you don't have a reader, you can bribe them. Sometimes I pay my kids to read books. Sometimes with video game time, sometimes with friend time, and sometimes with cold, hard cash. Listen, there are a lot of ways to earn money, and reading is not the worst idea I've heard, is all I'm saying.

In a perfect world, kids should have ten minutes of homework per grade level. So, twenty minutes for second grade, fifty minutes for fifth grade, etc. If your kid has no homework, figure out if that's what's supposed to be happening or if your kid is just super efficient at recess, and if they have a lot more than that, figure out if they're doing too much or if there's a concept they're struggling with. A large portion of my time parenting is determining if my kids are falling within a reasonable spectrum of school performance or if I need to call in reinforcements. The thought of a tutor makes the blood drain out of my children's faces, but they will try anything to get me to help them, and by "help them," I mean do their homework for them.

It starts with, "Can you just sit by me and keep me company?" and transitions into, "I need help with this one math problem," and pretty soon you're literally just doing their homework. My standard line is, "I already passed ____ grade." I have zero desire to go back, and I can't even remember how to multiply fractions or diagram a sentence at this point. If my children don't understand a concept, I encourage them to talk to the teacher about it. "The teacher needs to know that you don't understand." My overarching strategy with kids and homework is to empower them to get it done themselves. Sometimes that means sitting by them and asking them questions as they try to figure it out. Sometimes it means googling the concept with them and helping them get the tools they need to figure it out. If they're younger, it might mean emailing the teacher, but if they're older, then it means suggesting that they email the teacher, check the teacher's website, or google it themselves.

A word about the most dreaded of all the homework: projects. I'm sorry, Mom and Dad, for that salt map of Ohio you had to help me with, and the cassette tape recording of "Interview with Loki" you helped me make, and for that diorama we built together.

Middle school is awesome because you're basically done with projects. The only thing a middle schooler needs from you is to go out and buy poster board and any other supplies and also possibly take their technology away so they can focus.

In elementary school, it's still an all-play with the projects. You can always tell which projects were actually done by kids and which ones were done by a mom with a Michael's gift card and the Pinterest app. I offer ideas and supplies, but then I leave the projects to my kids, so for instance, my kid's turkey centerpiece for the Thanksgiving feast looks like he made it with his feet, but at least he did it himself.

This year, the night before the holiday feast at school, when they decorate the cafeteria in red and green and all the parents force themselves to eat off Styrofoam trays and squish into cafeteria tables and benches, Elliott came to me and said, "I need a pinecone."

"For what?" I asked.

"I have to decorate it for the meal." Glad I'm sending my kids to school so they can learn the fine art of tablescapes. We live in Georgia, so to locate a pinecone all you have to do is step outside.

He found one, but I had to take Evie to tumbling, so I told him to decorate it and ask Ana if he needed help. Ana's crafty. She likes glitter and doesn't break out in hives when she walks into Michael's.

My husband checked on them later and asked, "Why is the pinecone blue?"

"He told me he needed to paint a pinecone! He didn't say what for!" Ana yelled.

Elliott looked at the blue pinecone, picked it up, and threw it in the trash. "The pinecone was optional."

The next day, Alex and I met the kids in the cafeteria for our big meal and looked at the alpine pinecone displays. Parents had lovingly swathed their pinecones in flocking to look like real snow. There were pinecone winter wonderland creatures that looked straight out of *Rudolph the Red-Nosed Reindeer*. I've never been so glad my kid threw homework in the trash.

Stop doing your kid's homework. Calm the heck down. If they fail, better to fail a test in sixth grade than in tenth. Better to fail an eighth-grade exam than the SAT.

One of my kids refused to study or do homework. We begged; this kid refused. We grounded; the kid slammed doors. It was awful. My darling child felt like we were nagging constantly, and we felt like if we didn't, the child would flunk out. We tried hiring a tutor. It didn't help. I felt like all we were doing was fighting, so I asked our therapist what to do, and she said to make a deal that we wouldn't bring up homework for a grade period, and if at the end the grades were fine, then great. But if the grades were not fine, then that gave us permission to step back in. My kid agreed to this arrangement, excited that we'd stop nagging and convinced life would be utterly fabulous without us hovering.

At the end of the grade period, my baby had failed several classes and was in danger of being held back. I mean, I was thinking about getting "I told you so" tattooed to the tip of my tongue.

It was an awful period, but it taught an important lesson. SuperKid realized you can't blow off everything after all, and maybe some of the guidelines and reminders weren't so bad. So, we stepped back in, tightened the reins, and helped this kid pull up all the grades. The kid made it, by a hair, and we haven't had too many problems with grades since.

We figured it was better to learn this lesson before you're playing for keeps, before it really matters, than later, when colleges are looking and it matters a lot. Now my kid manages homework and studies mostly without me asking. We've come a long way. Sometimes failure is the best lesson you can give a kid.

5 WAYS TO TALK WITH TEACHERS

If you homeschool and you are the teacher, then I'm pretty sure the best way to effectively communicate with yourself is at a day spa. Call it a faculty meeting. Treat thyself. For the rest of us, here are some suggestions:

1. Find opportunities to respond with positive feedback. Our teachers do so much, but if we're not careful, we only contact them when we have a problem. If they send a weekly schedule that says they're doing a cool project or your kid comes home excited about a book you love, drop them an email and thank them.
2. Remember your kid is one of twenty-some kids in the class and cut the teacher some slack.
3. Believe the best about the teacher's intentions and start conversations by asking questions and listening to his or her perspective.
4. If you have an issue, start with the teacher before going to the principal. If you don't feel heard, then you can widen the conversation, but start with the courtesy of the direct approach.
5. If your kid comes home with a horrifying tale, take it seriously and believe them but consider that there could be some "lost in translation" going on and talk to the teacher and other parents at the school to get the full picture before freaking out.

10

Go Team Win the Sportsball!

Lighten Up About Activities

"You're gonna need a bigger boat."
—*Jaws*

When Alex and I were newlyweds, we swore we'd never get a minivan. "No minivan is in our prenup!" we'd joke to friends. We were kidding. We didn't have a prenup. In the event of divorce, neither of us had anything worth fighting over, and we'd already agreed we'd rather just kill each other. Less cleanup. I've seen *Dexter* and think I know where I can get some plastic sheeting.

But wait, this part isn't about murder; it's about minivans. While I did have a near-death experience in a minivan, the driver of the truck that slammed into me wasn't actually trying to kill me. Probably?

Anyway, two months into parenting our preemie, we ate humble pie (tastes like chicken!) and bought a minivan. That one got decimated by aforesaid truck, but did we take that off-ramp from the universe? Nope, we went out and bought the exact same minivan, only used and crappier than the first one.

We don't even have a fancy van. The fancy ones almost make up for being minivans. You might be embarrassed to drive it, but when you get out and show your skeptical friends, you can demonstrate things like, "Look how the back opens on its own using a psychic link they install at the dealership! It'll play whatever music I want by simply intuiting my current mood! And the seats are made of baby seal! Ooh, so soft." Ours has none of that, and I'm pretty sure the used one we bought had someone else's bloodstain on the seat belt. Or maybe it was ketchup. It was ketchup, okay?

I've spent the last twelve years explaining to kids, friends, and the intrepid car-line workers at school how to open and close manual doors, because our van is the last of its kind, in a world of automation. The doors stick and teachers and kids stare helplessly at them, waiting for them to open like everyone else's doors. No one moves. They think something is malfunctioning, and everyone starts gesturing to me. Is there a button to push? A voice command? I climb out of the van in my dirty jammies and flip-flops jammed over fuzzy socks, braless and ashamed, and yank on the handle till it opens. Everyone gives me pitying stares. "She has to use the handle on her van," they cluck sadly. Someone plays Sarah McLachlan in the background and organizes a telethon.

Whether you're a fancy car person or you Flintstone your way around town, as your kids get older and they start getting into activities, their gear increases along with the size of their butts. If you think you have enough space in your vehicle, you're wrong unless you drive the Scoobymobile. My disgusting van seats seven, with one of those seats taken by a humanoid monster made entirely from crumbs, and it is too small when I shove in one million swim team boys, their fins, snorkels, towels, bags, and water bottles. And get comfortable, because you're going to spend roughly 81 percent of your awake time in that van.

Whilst astride my very high horse, I once told myself that my kids would only have one activity each. We wouldn't be like these frenzied parents constantly dragging their kids to various sports things, nosirree. These days, as we drag our kids to various sports things every day, I realize that even though we do limit the activities, we still have three kids and there are only two of us, so it's a juggling routine of who needs to be where and when. We've had to divide and conquer, with Alex on field sports and me on the inside stuff like swimming and tumbling, but sometimes even that doesn't work. And then you throw in the extra stuff, like, "Mom! I made the science/running/chorus team at school and we just have these twelve practices and competitions and you need to sign up to bring snacks." I've given up trying to get into a routine. There is no routine. Each day comes at you like a fire hose, and you have to just let it hit you in the face.

I used to wonder why my parents stared at the TV watching mind-numbing shows every night when I was growing up, but now I do exactly that because at the end of every day, working all day then racing around town in my minivan to sportsball, I'm an empty droid capable only of snickering à la Beavis and Butt-Head as Jimmy Fallon smashes raw eggs on his forehead.

You will try to schedule everything, and sometimes you will fail. You will race around town, and you will leave a kid somewhere accidentally. Someday you'll forget snacks. Your kids can remember their own dang water bottles. Don't try to show up to everything. It's impossible. Check as many boxes as you can and leave the rest.

I look at activities as opportunities for kids to learn new skills, meet new people, develop character, and keep busy and out of trouble. We aren't trying to go pro or make the Olympics around here.

How the Heck Did I Become a Cheer Mom? And Other Existential Crises

In spite of your best efforts to indoctrinate your spawn to certain activities, they will make their own choices, possibly falling in love with your sports nemesis. Lighten up and remember that you aren't the one who has to play. You just have to show up and try to yell the right things without embarrassing your kid.

I am the world's worst soccer mom. I hate grass. I hate sports. I hate being outside and sweating. I stand on the sidelines griping about mosquitos and armpits while the other parents cheer supportively.

It's hot as balls here in Georgia, there are one billion biting bugs trying to get at my ankles and eyeballs, and you have to watch all the minutes of these games. I love swimming and cross-country for oh so many reasons, but one big one is that you give them your full concentration for the minutes or seconds they're racing, but then you're off the hook till the next one.

Not so with an entire soccer game, especially if they don't have many subs. This is where dark sunglasses can help, because as long as you keep your head pointed toward the field, you can lower your eyeballs, just your eyeballs, and take a sneak peek at your phone. Another option is to hold the phone up and pretend you're taking photos of your darling pumpkin when really, you're catching up on Twitter gossip. The parents around you will know, but hopefully they'll be cool and not out you to your little athlete.

I know. I sound super fun. I think with me, God had in mind more of an indoor, bookish sort who could read about other people experiencing the outdoors from the comfort of a nice sofa.

After years of schlepping folding chairs to fields and trying to make small talk with other parents on the sidelines while my kids attempted to remember which goal was theirs, I finally got to give it a rest. First one, then another child tried and quit soccer and my third and final child decided against giving it a go. I breathed a sigh of relief. It was finished.

And then something happened that made me long for the days of soccer. My youngest, a wee kindergartner at the time, decided she desperately needed to try cheerleading.

What.

There's something about parenting that makes us confront our deepest, darkest fears, and I have the fear of athletics AND ginormous girly bows, and here was a sport that combined both. We were facing a childhood filled with grosgrain ribbon and herkies and pyramids.

As I filled out the online form, I felt my insides shrivel. This sport comes with more enthusiasm than any other. Cheerleading is the choice of perky people who love their teams and feel things like loyalty and school spirit and such. Clearly, I was doomed. I wasn't even sure I was capable of woohoo-ing unsarcastically, although I'd do anything to try to support my daughter. (Though I secretly nursed some healthy vengeance against her for putting me through this.)

I remember a cheer that always bothered me when I was in school:

Cheerleaders: R-O-W-D-I-E THAT'S THE WAY WE
SPELL ROWDY, ROWDY, LET'S GET ROWDY WOO-WOO-WOO!

Me: But it's not. That's not how you spell it. Do they not know? DO THEY NOT KNOW?!?

I had it on good authority that I was going to raise nerds. My husband was the president of the chess club at his little private school, where I picture them all in matching argyle and knee pants. (This is probably not true, but let me have my fantasy. The chess part was real, and he is so hot to me in my mind. Take my pawn again, Nerd King. You're the man.)

I had glasses, braces, zits, and a varsity letter in show choir. So, you know, the nerd thing for my kids seemed like a reasonable assumption. I was hoping to throw in some kind of woodwind instrument and a band uniform involving a ruffled dickie to seal the deal, but no. Now I was looking at pom-poms and spankies. (My husband just informed me that cheering seems awfully similar to show choir and jazz hands. Now I'm questioning everything and need chocolate, a fuzzy blanket, and some tap shoes.)

My child was going to be a cheerleader. (*Faints, stands back up, watches* Bring It On, *faints again.*)

Just as the shaking in my hands from signing her up ebbed a bit, I got an email in my inbox about . . . football. *That's silly. Nobody here does that thing.* Football? Please. I've spent years trying lackadaisically to understand that game and I never will. I watch the Superbowl for Beyoncé and Beyoncé alone. Why was I getting an email welcoming my child to the world of footballlll OH MY GOSH, CHEERLEADERS CHEER FOR FOOTBALL GAMES, HOT DAMN.

Cheering doesn't happen in a vacuum. The girls are cheering FOR something. For boys. I would be spending every Saturday on a football field watching my daughter shake her booty for a bunch of padded-up peewee players.

I started wondering if she'd forgive me for screaming random epithets about THE PATRIARCHY!

Me: GIRLS! YOU DON'T HAVE TO CHEER FOR BOYS! CHEER FOR YOURSELVES! WHO'S CHEERING FOR YOU, GIRLS!?!

Evie: I don't know that crazy woman over there whipping her bra through the air. Weird.

This is what was going through my head as I prepared for cheer season, I mean football season. I didn't even watch *Friday Night Lights* or *Varsity Blues*. (I thought *Friday Night Lights* was about theater openings and marquees. True story.)

I was completely intimidated because this was not my lane. My lane was more of a literal lane, in a swimming pool.

But. It was my daughter's lane, and even though I couldn't be in the lane, I was going to be at the end of the lane cheering wildly for my little cheerleader. Melanie Dale, Cheer Mom.

If you are a cheer mom or a cheerleader, forgive me. It's not you, it's me. I tried to adjust and be as awesome as possible. It worked out okay. I brought snacks and learned to tie bows and be the sports bra of supportiveness. Don't give up on me. Please be my friend.

This is what we do as parents, isn't it? We support our kids and consequently end up thrown into new situations with other parents who intimidate the heck out of us as we act like we know what we're doing. So, let me be the first to say, "Hi. I don't know what I'm doing. I'm intimidated and a total dork and scared of blowing it with all of you."[12]

Evie finally did decide to try soccer, to the utter joy of her daddy. After a few years of her screaming cheers into a megaphone directly into my inner ear, she wanted to give soccer a go, while still tumbling at the cheer gym every week. Somehow, I went from hating soccer and cheer to having both in my life, and then Ana started lacrosse, which I'll never, ever understand. There are so many rules, and I can't seem to repress the urge to flinch every time they whip that ball near her head. But I like how badass the girls look in their goggles and mouth guards. I may not always like what my kids do, but I sure do like them.

Sportsball Isn't Everything

As a kid, I tried soccer, basketball, and cross-country, but I was terrifically awful at all sports, with the possible exception, if we're being generous, of summer league swim team. So, as a drama nerd who was talented at zero sports, I don't want to give the impression that sports are everything. I feel the opposite. Keeping our kids busy and out of our butt cracks is where my heart truly is. While my peers were earning trophies back in the '80s

---

12 I originally published this section as an essay called "Cheer Mom," for my friend Bronwyn Lea's blog, at https://bronlea.com/2016/05/25/cheer-mom/.

when people actually earned them for more than participating, I was taking cake decorating and cartooning classes, competing in creative writing contests, and attending one million music lessons, which culminated in thousands of hours of show choir and drama club rehearsals. If it didn't involve muscles or balls, then I was your girl. Spanish club, Student Council, and intramural art club, bring it on. Tennis or softball, bring it off.

Before your parents could just humblebrag about you on Facebook to their friends and relatives, we had our local paper, the source of all noteworthy accomplishments. Each week, we'd open up the paper, hoping for a mention of our drama club presentation of Bertolt Brecht's *Mother Courage* or a photo from the Cotillion Club where we learned to dance the fox-trot in white gloves. But no. Week in, week out, we'd open it up to the grappling rears of sweaty wrestlers and football players. Sportsy kids seemed to get all the press, and the rest of us existed in their shadows. Hard to believe, considering how riveting my life as a nerd really was.

In sixth grade, I represented our school at the county spelling bee. My parents were so proud. It was held on the stage in our high school's auditorium, and sixth-, seventh-, and eighth-grade students from schools across the county showed up to compete. The judges gave us a practice round to get out the jitters. (Yes, Chad, public spelling is scary. I'd like to see you try it.) When it was my turn, I strode to the front of the stage.

"Your word is SMILE." *Okay, practice round, easy words we don't even have to think about. I've got this.*

"S-L-I-M-E," I confidently spoke into the mic. The judges looked at each other and the audience tittered softly.

"Would you like to try that again?" The judge smiled. She S-M-I-L-E-D.

"S-L-I-M-E. It's S-L-I-M-E." What was going on? Did the microphone not work?

"Your word is SMILE," the judge tried one more time. My mind raced. What was I missing? S-L-I-M-E.

S-LLLLLL-OH. Yikes.

"S-M-I-L-E." The judges looked relieved, the audience openly laughed, and I slunk back to my seat. Who says you need sports to feel the harsh pressure of competition? I was mortified but determined to redeem myself, which I did, finishing in the top five and advancing to regionals.

I didn't want to pigeonhole my kids into any one thing, so when they were younger, we let them try everything. I attended weekly music classes, we went to story time at the library, we tried sports camps, art camps, cooking classes, sewing classes, and science clubs.

Don't worry if your kid doesn't want to do anything or wants to do too much. We have both kinds of kids. Eventually, they found their thing. With one of our kids we have to scale back and make sure there's enough free play time because some kids want to overschedule themselves and also you, because you are the driver of the minivan. Another one of our kids didn't want to do anything ever and was content spending all day every day on the couch moping around. That's also not going to fly. We gave the ultimatum: choose an activity or we will choose one for you. We had to spend about a year choosing for them before they took care of it and picked something.

We've had to learn to lighten up about the activities our kids love. Our son is an avid gamer, and every time I see another blog post about how video games are ruining The Youth, I can't help but feel a little nervous. Thankfully, he loves reading, too, and his commitment to swim team keeps him busy. The pool is the one place he cannot access tech. My husband helps me lighten up in this area by reminding me that these days playing video games doesn't mean you'll live in the basement for the rest of your life. Esports is a rapidly expanding industry, and "video game designer" is a fantastic career option.

Keep Them the Right Amount of Busy

As my kids got older, I talked with parents a little ahead of me and they all gave me the same advice: "You've gotta keep them busy." This was the direct opposite of everything I'd heard during the early years, when we're supposed to focus on free play and creativity and letting kids be kids. But as my babes grew up, I realized the wisdom in this. They'd spend more and more time in their rooms, headphones on, locked away from the world, or in the basement in front of video games, headphones on, locked away from the world. We still want them to have downtime, but too much downtime leads to isolation and sadness.

So, as they get older and develop The Puberty, we need to keep them active and tire them out. Find a sport they like, get them in a class, audition for the school play—whatever it is, get them out and active and interacting in healthy ways with their peers. My kids leave for their practices pissy and come home with rosy cheeks and a better attitude.

Working hard and pursuing the things we love lightens up our lives and helps our family function happier and healthier. For some reason, when we have unlimited hours of free time, we tend to fart it away staring at screens or wandering aimlessly around the house with our hand in a bag of chips, but when we're actively engaged in things we care about, it helps our work ethic, and we become sharper and more productive. We still have free time, but we need balance.

Everything in moderation, and that goes for activities, too. We need enough in their lives to organize our schedule a bit and hold us accountable to the outside world and find some friends. But not so many that you never have downtime, have to be in five places at once, and your kid is having panic attacks every Sunday night in anticipation of the week.

Sports and activities have been a big help for our kids, giving our family some much-needed structure, discipline, and healthy goals and relationships. But if you let them, these activities will take over your life pretty quickly. Figure out how much time and money you're willing and able to commit and learn to set boundaries to guard your family as needed. Some of these teams can get destructively competitive. No one wants a forty-year-old getting red-faced and apoplectic in your six-year-old's cherubic face because he couldn't remember which goal was his. Find the team or activity that fits your family's and child's personality. And if you know you take sports too seriously, calm down, invest in a stress ball, and don't be that guy.

I'm bad at quitting things and still feel guilty over quitting piano after ten years of lessons, but I remind myself all the time that it's okay to quit sometimes. It's not really quitting. It's homing in on their passion. I don't want to raise quitters, so we make them finish out a season or the camp or classes. They have to finish the investment, but if after putting in the time, they decide that they hate it, it's okay to walk away and try something else. And it's okay to go back to it and try again, although I have my limits.

One of my girls tried dance two different times. The first time I sat in the lobby and watched while she licked the mirror, rolled around on the floor, and distracted the teacher. She decided she hated dance, and I couldn't wait to get out of there. A few years later, she wanted to try again, so I forced myself to go back to that studio. At first, she seemed happy to be there, but slowly her enthusiasm waned, she decided she definitely didn't want to do a recital, and we quit once again. But this time, I told her this was it. If she quit dance again, there would be no going back. She nodded solemnly, and we walked away à la Angela Bassett from that burning car in *Waiting to Exhale*.

Boredom Is an Important Developmental Tool. Let It Wash over You.

In the chapter on activities and how wonderful and important they are, let me end with a passionate defense of boredom. Boredom is so important, and while we do the sports and the activities and the video games and we wear out our kids with all the things, we also work hard to leave space for boredom. These days it's hard to find the time and discipline to let our minds wander, but it's so important. We need to cultivate time for our kids to stare out a window, mess with a jumble of art supplies, create a blanket fort, or build a nest in the backyard. I'm usually annoyed at the beginning of their boredom, but if I refuse to save them from it, eventually their creativity will kick in and they'll create a whole new world, make something with their hands, or find a neighbor to play with. Sometimes in utter desperation, my older kids will fall asleep. Like their growing bodies don't know how to handle the lack of input, and they just power down. That's good, too. Everyone needs rest. Boredom saves lives.

When it comes to my kids' boredom, I assume no responsibility. During my own childhood, I lucked out and actually enjoyed reading, so I spent the vast majority of my time with my nose in a book. Therefore, I understand my kids' boredom exactly zero percent and provide no help whatsoever. When my kids are bored, I become an extra snotty Hermione Granger, lording my love of books over the helpless Harrys and Rons of the world.

Them: I'm bored.
Me: Only boring people are bored.

Them: I'm bored.
Me: Here's a chore. There. Fixed it.

Them: I'm bored.
Me: Get a book.
Them: Reading is boring.
Me: I don't understand these words you're stringing together.

Them: I'm bored.
Me: I feel sorry for you. I'm never bored because there's an adventure in every book.

Them: I'm bored.
Me: I'm not a cruise director.

Them: I'm bored.
Me: Good. Boredom is super important to brain development. Hashtag science.

I offer no craft ideas. I will not entertain you. If I'm free, I might play the occasional board game or offer to work a puzzle, which my kids consider equally as boring as doing nothing. I do not catch or throw balls. I eschew balls of any kind. In the summer I take them to the pool, but what they choose to do there is up to them. I'm reading. In the winter I'll stoke the fire in the fireplace, but what they choose to do in front of it is up to them. I'm reading.

17 THINGS YOU NEED TO SURVIVE SPORTSBALL SEASON

1. Collapsible wagon for wheeling all your crap across fields.
2. Camp chairs, and don't be dumb like us and throw away the bags with handles. You'll want those handles as you lug the chairs everywhere.
3. Bleacher seat with comfy pad to protect against Flat Butt, preferably with lower back support. Cup holders are a bonus.
4. Ginormous Yeti filled with coffee.
5. Extra water bottles because your kids will lose five water bottles a month. Do not invest in a fancy water bottle with a monogrammed cover. Rookie mistake.
6. Dark sunglasses so you can pretend not to make eye contact with the other sportsball parents who are screaming at their kids from the sidelines. Also, when you wear sunglasses, you can still check your phone while pretending to watch every second of your precious baby's game.

7. Layers. We leave the house when it's pitch-black and freezing, then by game or meet time it's burning lava hot.

8. Sunscreen, because you haven't truly parented until you've ended up with a weird tan line from all-day sun exposure on your Sports Mom tee.

9. Collapsible tent. Make friends with tall parents to help with setup and takedown. I am short and no help with this.

10. Clip-on chair umbrella, for when the tent is too much.

11. Visor or hat.

12. Snacks. Pack what you think you'll need, then double it.

13. Bug spray if you live in a primordial hell swamp like I do.

14. Obviously, all their gear, and the sooner you can train them to pack it themselves the better. ("Oh, you're mad you forgot your water bottle? I'd be mad, too. But I remembered mine right here. Maybe next time you'll remember. I believe in you!")

15. Sharpie, for labeling everything. They get a new team shirt? Sharpie their name in the tag immediately. New water bottle? Sharpie. And of course, for us swimmer parents, we have to Sharpie our kids' races directly on their skin.

16. A book. Bring two if it's an all-day thing because I've run out of words mid-meet before and then you have to talk to people.

17. Cash, because at any given moment someone is collecting for a coach's gift, someone needs something at the concession stand, they're selling new car magnets, or for drugs in the parking lot. I don't know drugs, but is it a cash-based situation?

11

Celebrate Good Times, or Don't

Lighten Up About Making Memories

"Driver picks the music. Shotgun shuts his cakehole."
—Supernatural

We have to talk about all the public pooping happening in our national parks. Well, we don't have to, no one's making us, but let's. A few weeks ago, my dad sent me an article, because for reasons unknown (they're totally known), people send me this kind of content on the regular (yes, that's a poop pun). Apparently, improperly stashed human feces are a growing problem on our public lands.

If you can't clean up after yourself, your turds are going to ruin it for the rest of us, and according to this very important fecal-related article, that's exactly what's happening.[13] This is reason 5,427 why I don't go camping.

Even as a solidly anti-camping family, we still get ourselves

---

13 Gray Chapman, "America's National Parks Are Being Ruined by Human Poop," *Vice*, October 3, 2018. https://www.vice.com/en_us/article/9kvkm7/americas-national -parks-are-being-ruined-by-human-poop.

into trouble. Several years ago, against our better judgment, to try to impress someone, we attempted to go hiking with one of our kids in Colorado. The specific park and specific child shall not be named in order to protect the super guilty.

Unless your middle name is Metamucil, travel always causes a disturbance in the Force (you know what I'm talking about), so dragging a child to Colorado while said child was also recovering from the flu was ill-conceived. To then take the child up a small mountain with no bathroom bordered on monstrous. No one ever said we were Parents of the Year.

Halfway up the mountain, while trying to keep up with the altitude-acclimated dear one we were trying to impress, my child announced that a bathroom was needed posthaste. Alex sighed and started back down the mountain to the parking lot while I soldiered up the mountain with the rest of our party. When we made it to the top, we waited, and waited, and waited, and started worrying about Alex and child. Just when my worry reached a critical apex, I saw them trudging toward us, looking . . . you know when you can see it in someone's eyes? It's like a combination of shame and thinly veiled desperation. Alex looked at risk for flinging himself off the mountain altogether, and as they got closer, I smelled why.

On the way down the mountain, child could no longer hold it and was forced to release the offending poo into the wild. The path was steep, and Alex had to anchor child by holding on to a tree and stabilizing our beloved with his fatherly arms. Unfortunately, it was a number-three situation, and upon pressure release, the poo exploded horizontally, covering the ground below, nearby rocks, Alex's shoes, and child's pant legs. The splash zone was relentless and thorough. Just then, triumphant hikers making their way back down after enjoying the scenic views from the top happened upon them and experienced the unfortunate mid-mountain scenery. "Nothing beats the view from the top," and their trek down proved that aphorism exponentially. Alex could do nothing but nod, as one hand gripped the tree and the other hand gripped the child.

I had handed Alex a half-used travel packet of tissues, and he used the approximately one and a half modest squares to wipe as much off their hands as possible. From this moment, there was nowhere to go but up, so up they went, rejoining us at the top, wild-eyed and haunted from the memories of what just happened.

We don't hike anymore. The terror is still too fresh.

Ah, memories. Some are worth remembering more than others.

When you become a parent, all of a sudden you're supposed to turn into an archivist, saving and cataloging every precious memory from your little snowflake. For the first child, you do your darnedest, gluing photos in albums and writing down stats like first tooth, first step, and first first. But as your kid gets older and if you add any new kids into the mix, your best intentions collide with actually trying to live your life and you end up with the Cabinet of Regret, this piece of furniture in my home dedicated to empty albums and loose photos piled together with the best of intentions. Or here in this digital age, maybe like me, you have a folder on your computer called "Pictures" that contains thousands of unsorted photos from the last decade.

When they go to school it gets even worse, because suddenly every day they're like mules coming home with backpacks filled with reams of papers. How do you know what to save? Are you supposed to get excited about every handprint? Do you need to rent a storage unit for all the memories? In addition to your new archival duties, you're also expected to take your kids on vacations and to the zoo and various outings. These trips go through the following phases: anticipation of the trip, trying to keep everyone calm and avoid public scenes during the trip, post-trip exhaustion, and vowing never to leave the house again.

We gotta lighten up about the memories.

Stop Saving Everything Like You Work at the National Archives

I should warn you: I grew up in a home with very little sentimentality. After I went to college, my parents moved, stored my stuff in the basement, turned my room into the guest room, and painted it my least favorite colors. The second I had a house of my own, they boxed up all my stuff and handed it to me to deal with, which is why I have a bunch of Young Authors and Illustrators Contest awards piled next to my desk right now. I may never be a *New York Times* bestselling author, but my books from grade school got blue ribbons.

This is why I throw away most of the stuff my kids bring home. When they're younger, you have to protect their sweet feelings and toss things when they turn their backs, but as they get older, you can shove things directly in the trash can without them batting an eye. I open their folders while standing over the kitchen trash can. If it's a good sample of their grade-level work, a compelling essay, or the teacher wrote something nice on it, I'll set it in a pile. Or for the younger ones, if there's a handprint. Everything else goes directly in the trash. I have a three-stack drawer bin in the kitchen and once I have my final sorted piles, I toss each kid's savable papers in their "special box" and am done with it. At the end of each school year, or more realistically the day they go back to school in the fall because I like to procrastinate, I pull out the papers from the special bins and put them in deep storage in the basement. I'm making a big plastic bin for each kid that I'll plop at their house someday when they finally move out and get a basement of their own.

I should admit here that I save my kids' teeth in a shoebox in my closet like I'm a serial killer, so I throw away school papers but keep human remains. I'm not sure why. Those little teeth are a part of them, but I don't really have an endgame here. Someday when they're adults, what am I going to do, present them with their baggie full of smelly old teeth? I've seen some scary tooth-related projects on Etsy, but no thank you. These little guys will not be sewn into a creepy, grinning doll.

I've thought through my logic with the teeth-saving, and there are some holes. Like, where do I draw the line? If my kid needs his appendix out someday, will I save that in a canopic jar, à la the ancient pharaohs? I've watched *The Mummy* movies and things don't go so well for Brendan Fraser. (Fun fact: Evie is named after Evelyn from *The Mummy*. A lot of people around here give their kids family names or biblical names, and when they ask me where I got Evie's, I have to explain my love of monsters.)

Shut Up, Pinterest, We Don't Have to Celebrate Everything

If you're a crafty person, that's fantastic. You log in to Pinterest and craft all the fabulous things. You make magic out of Mason jars and discarded pieces of burlap. You create homemade confections and know how to wield a pastry bag without the frosting exploding out the top. Do your thing. But even you probably have your limits, and for the rest of us, that limit is the second we open the pantry.

I've survived the onslaught of crafty parenting demands three ways: saying no, cheating, and delegating.

Saying No

First, we don't have to celebrate everything. It's getting out of hand. Did you celebrate the one hundredth day of school when you were a kid by dressing up like a senior citizen and eating one hundred M&Ms? Neither did I, but our kids do. And this year I saw a grade celebrating the fiftieth day of school, too. A world of nope. Not everything is worth celebrating.

My daughter asked me when we were going to have mother-daughter craft time, and I replied, "Never." She looked shocked. Somewhere along the line she'd gotten it in her head that that's what moms and daughters do. Not this one. I told her I love doing lots of things with her. We play games, we read books, sometimes we even cook easy stuff, but I will never be the mom who works on a craft project with her. I'm happy to get her supplies for her own projects, but this is not an all-play. It's okay to say no, and if I'm going to calm the heck down, this is one area I have to avoid.

Cheating

I don't have the bandwidth to make a million cutesy memories with my kids, but even at my level of halfheartedness, I've accidentally created traditions that my kids look forward to. When I asked them what they were looking forward to at Christmas, they said gingerbread houses. These contraptions are high maintenance messes. I want no part of it. But every year, apparently, I impulse-buy those premade kits whenever I'm at Walmart or Trader Joe's or wherever and my kids love building them on their own. They assemble their little prefab gingerbread houses, and I snap their pictures and somewhere along the way, I guess it became a tradition. A beautiful holiday tradition that involves zero baking and stirring on my part. Kids don't care. They just want to stick candy on cookie pieces or frost cupcakes or whatever. They really don't care if you work too much and don't make time to lovingly sift treats from scratch.

The other day I bought my son a fancy cinnamon roll from our swanky bakery in town, and when he took a bite, I asked him excitedly, "Is it amazing?" "Eh," he shrugged. "Your homemade ones are better." I was confused. My cinnamon rolls? I don't bake—wait, did he mean the can I whack on the counter and split apart, bake, and glob icing on? The whack-a-can rolls? Those are better than the fancy bakery?!?

I have cracked the code on parenting: less is more, and they don't notice where stuff comes from.

Speaking of icing, here's another cheat I do to make it seem like I'm trying harder than I am. Instead of using a pastry bag with the little tips where you have to clean everything and instead you throw it in the back of the pantry and try not to make direct eye contact with it, you can make swirly frosting on cupcakes that's super easy. Spoon store-bought icing into a sandwich bag, seal it, and cut a tiny corner off one side. Squeeze the icing out and swirl it onto cupcakes or cookies. Throw the whole thing in the trash when you're done. Thank you and good night. Cheaters sometimes win.

Delegating

When your kids get old enough, you can start delegating to them for the memory making. If your middle schoolers want cupcakes for their class, awesome. Buy a mix, show them how to work the oven, and let them handle it.

Just keep passing projects on to your kids to sort out. Print out photos and hand them to your kids and let them slide them into albums. I do this with my kids' camp photos every summer, and they love it. Older kids can go through their own school papers and decide what they want to save. You can be quality control and make sure they aren't throwing away something good.

My mom loves to bake, and now that she and my dad are retired, she doesn't have anyone to bake for, so she told me to sign up for baked goods and let her do it. I have to force down my natural fight-or-flight tendency when it comes to cookie signups, but now my mom gets to do what she does best, love people with sugar and flour, and all I have to do is sign up and drop stuff off. And no, I do not take credit. I have integrity. I can't believe you even thought that.

Confession: that same lovely woman did my trigonometry homework one time junior year of high school. She was a math major in college, and I didn't see the point of trig for a career in the performing arts, so she started out just "showing me how to do it" and then got so intoxicated with making the numbers her bizitches that she finished the whole page and handed it back to me sheepishly. In her defense, she made sure I understood the concept first. What? I was helping her. She needed trig homework more than I did.

Let people help you. We think we have to do everything ourselves, but we don't. Ask for help. Call in reinforcements. Phone a friend. And then when it's your turn, step up and help someone else.

Birthday Party Etiquette

Okay, let's talk about birthday parties. I feel, as a society, that we are out of control about the celebrating. This is true of gender reveal parties as well, but since I assume you've already either done or not done that at this point and are well into celebrating your kid, I won't go back and beat a dead horse.

But birthday parties are out of hand. If Grandma may have the floor for a hot minute, I'd like to share a few ways we can lighten up about birthday parties.

First, you don't have to throw a party every year. I know—gasp—what kind of evil parent am I? I don't know how you were raised, but we didn't get a party every year. My general rule of thumb is about every other year when they're young, and then thirteen, sixteen, and I dunno, maybe eighteen but probably not because hopefully we'll be throwing a graduation party that year, and kids don't need all the constant celebrating or they'll think they're royalty, and I'm not raising Sophia the First.

Anyway, on the off years, I let them pick something and invite a friend or two. We go see a movie or grab dinner. Simple, non-festive. My son has gone a different route and typically likes to celebrate every year with a couple friends playing video games all night. Fine. Done.

Now for the party years, you can keep it simple. Kids will not remember if all the paper goods were on theme. They won't care if the cake is store-bought. The main thing is keeping them entertained and fed. One year I invited Evie's preschool class to TCBY after school and paid for everyone to go through the line. They ate, went home, and I had zero clean-up. One year I bought the whole party Chick-fil-A kids' meals, swapped the toys inside for ice creams for everyone, let them play in the playland, and I had zero clean-up. One year I brought a cake to Evie's tumbling gym and they ate, went home, and I had zero clean-up. Ana had a pool party at our neighborhood pool, and I had zero clean-up. I think my favorite year was when she was obsessed with Starbucks, so I reserved the little conference room they had, bought everyone lattes, and plopped baskets of dollar-store makeup and hair accessories in the middle of the table, and they gave each other crazy makeovers and we took pictures. And then they went home, and I had zero clean-up.

You see the theme emerging. Zero clean-up is important, because once everyone leaves, you want to collapse and pretend like other people's children don't exist and that you don't have to now spend the next three days threatening your kid to write thank-you notes for all the bags and bags of wonderful things they've already lost or broken.

If you want to rent live animals, hand paint themed nametags, and invite the entire school over to linger for seven hours in your home, by all means do it and invite my kid, thanks in advance. But you don't have to.

When my first kid turned one, I served both chicken curry and beef tips, made a ginormous layer cake from scratch, and invited everyone I'd ever met. I'd kept my first kid alive for a whole year, and I wanted to celebrate. He has no memory of that entire event. I could've eaten a cupcake by myself and called it done.

Do whatever you want with birthdays, and for the love, don't feel pressure to do it a certain way. Some families simply go out to dinner together. Evie's birthday is two days before Christmas, and you cannot compete with Jesus. It is impossible to gather a quorum of friends that close to Christmas, so we pull something together right after Thanksgiving. Elliott's birthday has an uncanny knack for being either on Easter or Easter-adjacent. What is it with my kids observing the Church calendar with their entries into the world? So, we keep it pretty simple around here.

As for celebrating myself, I'm all over it. For Mother's Day last year, I took a family-sized bag of M&Ms, a bag of Doritos, and a bottle of champagne to our neighborhood pool and worked my way through them while reading a book by myself. When I turned forty, I cracked open a bottle of Lagavulin and watched *Nightmare on Elm Street* by myself. Celebrate thyself (because your kids might not).

My mom always made us incredible cakes and decorated them with five million different colors of homemade frosting using all the cake decorating tools. She was amazing. One year I had a party at the roller-skating rink (are you even an '80s kid if you didn't have a party at the skating rink?) and my dog Zak ate the wheel off my roller skate cake. At another birthday party, this one at the bowling alley (the '80s were big on birthday parties featuring rented footwear), all I remember is that I was trying out my first foray with leggings as pants and was very aware of my crotchular area the entire time. I didn't try that look again until this year, when the overconfidence that comes with middle age finally kicked in.

Whatever you decide to do about celebrating your kid, let me throw out my opinion on birthday party etiquette, because maybe we're not all on the same page. Obviously, we all blow it occasionally, and there's grace for that, but in general, if someone invites your kid to their party, RSVP by the deadline. If you've ever experienced the parental rage over a dejected child because no one bothered to respond and hardly anyone showed up for their party, you know what I mean.

You don't have to attend every party you're invited to, and there's a time in there right around kindergarten where you'll reach a party saturation level that's out of control and you'll be looking for toys on the clearance rack at Ross or putting together bags from the dollar store so you don't have to second mortgage your home. So, it's okay to say no. What's not okay, unless your kid is sick or an emergency happens, is to blow someone off. You think it's just you, but if everyone does that, you're left with a kid with an empty party and one more thing to work out in therapy later in life.

Better in Hindsight

A lot of memory making is better in hindsight. By two years after our trip to Disney, I could look back and remember the good times. But during the trip I felt like a warden making a prisoner transfer. I had to keep my inmates locked down in the bus while we got to where we were going and could let them loose in the yard. I just had to keep them from assaulting the general public or causing a scene.

At one point we were the family with the kid ripping up a bed of tulips at Epcot. My kids were more fascinated with the old-school phone booths they saw at the Biergarten restaurant in Germany at the World Showcase than the rides.

If you have more than two kids like we do, we've found it makes or breaks a trip to spring for a suite. We need some kind of second-room option, both because of how many beds we need and also because we need a spot to recover while the little ones fall asleep in the other room.

When we visited DC, I couldn't find an affordable suite option and didn't want to pay for or deal with adjoining hotel rooms, so I found an Airbnb two-bedroom apartment that was perfect. I cooked really easy dinners like spaghetti or mac and cheese, and Alex and I would sneak to the back bedroom and drink boxed wine while the kids watched TV and recovered from a day of togetherness walking miles in the 1,000 percent humidity.

When booking travel, know your limits. I am not a fun person. When I plan a family trip, I know I'm going to need a little space to get my head on straight at the end of the day. My three very different kids are going to need some flexibility to pursue their different interests. And we really don't need a lot of bells and whistles to make it exciting. A motel with all-you-can-eat cereal in the morning pretty much blows my kids' minds. We don't need much for the wow factor.

As for the difficulties of traveling with kids, those memories will fade, and when you look back, you'll mostly remember the good stuff. Which is a double-edged sword, because two years after our Disney trip, I forgot about the hard stuff, booked us to Universal Studios, and back we went.

13 SURVIVAL ITEMS YOU DON'T WANT TO VACAY WITHOUT

1. Change of clothes for everyone including you, because if they barf, they're probably barfing on you. This is especially important if you're transporting your kids in public, like on a plane, train, or bus.

2. Plastic bags for dirty clothes, vomit, diapers, shoes with poop on them, anything you don't want to smell for ten hours.

3. Noise-canceling headphones.

4. Fuzzy blanket and fourteen layers because the car will be anywhere from an ice box to a sauna as you try to navigate everyone's temperature needs. Make sure the kids have layers and blankets as well.

5. Book of questions for couples so when your partner is driving, gets bored, and says, "Talk to me," you don't have to struggle for something to say. I just keep asking Alex questions, and he unpacks his entire childhood, feelings about his career, and aspirations in life while I snuggle in my blanket, crooning, "Mm-hmm. Tell me more about that."

6. Earplugs.

7. Hand sanitizer for gross gas station bathrooms.

8. Clorox wipes.

9. Toilet paper. There's a rule that says you'll pass ten exits with perfectly stocked restrooms and stop at the one that's out of soap, toilet paper, and paper towels, with the faucet

that won't turn off and the maxi pad stuck to the side of the toilet.

10. Paper towels. You won't need them unless you forget them, so bring them to ward off spills and vomit.

11. Snacks. I pack a carton of Goldfish crackers and a stack of cups, plus Twizzlers for bribery when they get whiny. Also, bananas, apples, and clementines.

12. Lunch. Peanut butter or Nutella, loaf of bread, plastic knife, plates, and napkins. My kids are never hungry at the same time, so I come with an entire bag of lunch items and make sandwiches as needed. I hate superfluous stopping on trips. It's long enough, and the only relief you'll have from this nightmare on wheels is to arrive at your destination and put some space between everybody. If we're stopping, it's for gas and pee, and usually the forty-minute dump one of my kids has been saving all week for this one-holer out behind the gas station with the trash can lid attached to the key.

13. Only water to drink because sugary drinks make them pee more, and peeing more means an extra two thousand hours of drive time.

12

When Armpits Awaken

Lighten Up About Big Kids

"I'm scared to close my eyes; I'm scared to
open them. We're gonna die out here!"
—*The Blair Witch Project*

Yesterday my kid smelled like honey and breast milk. I think it must've been only yesterday, but maybe time is doing that wonky thing it does, since he's twelve and my desiccated boobs continue their slow slide to their final resting place somewhere in the vicinity of my waist. Over a decade has passed since I slathered him with Burt's Bees and rocked him in my glider until he passed out in a happy milk coma.

I used to rub my nose in his silky hair, breathing in his baby scent. I tried it the other day and gagged.

Me: When was the last time you showered?
Kid: Uhh . . .
Me: Go. Use shampoo. Don't forget your butt crack.

When my kids were little, I used all natural everything. I cloth-diapered and pureed homemade organic baby food. I drove forty-five minutes to a chicken farm for my very own free-range chicken carcass complete with intact neck hanging off the top. Looked like a very sad penis, but I drove that chicken penis home and basted the hell out of it. I composted with worms for my garden where I grew all our vegetables. I sewed my son jammies out of organic fabric I ordered off the internet. He looked like he'd joined some kind of culty secret society in the woods where they train small children to be assassins. Very cuddly, droopy-butt assassins.

I was concerned about the toxins and the artificial additives. My house smelled like lavender, and I felt the parental pride of knowing I was making crunchy granola choices for my pure-as-new-fallen-snow kids.

And then my kids got bigger.

One day I pulled out a fresh load of laundry from the dryer and it smelled sour. How could this be? I just washed it. It should smell like whatever all-natural soap I drizzled lovingly into the wash, but instead it smelled like all-natural feet. I plucked a sock out of the pile and came in for a closer sniff.

Holy mother of dragons. The sock smelled like it had been buried on a corpse found at the bottom of a dumpster on a pier at the marina. I rewashed the entire load, using extra hippie detergent and threw in a sanctimonious lecture for good measure. Hours later I pulled it out hopefully . . . still full-on corpse. My kids' socks could wake the dead.

I needed to up my laundry game. And maybe find something to waft around the house, like a church censer that could also purify my home of flatulence demons. I found myself strolling up and down the aisles at Target, searching for stronger products that would blow out the glandular stenches that were overtaking my home.

I started small, but it was a slippery slope.

Maybe this product will kill the odor. Maybe this one will decontaminate the room. If I empty a whole can of this into their shoes, will we finally be able to ride in the car together without a barf bag?

As I sprayed and doused and poured and slathered the blissful chemicals into our clothes, throughout the air, and on all major surfaces, I breathed deep the unnatural aromas of fake ocean mist and unrealistic meadow. I sent my kids to school with confidence. They would not be the smelly ones. (One of my kids didn't shower all last week and grew extremely irate when I forced the issue this week. Work in progress.)

Kid: (*points to armpit*) Mom, I think puberty happened.

Me: (*smells armpit*) YEP. (*Grabs deodorant and applies liberally.*)

Me: You gotta use this every day and cover it up.

Kid: It's so weird. I was playing and was like WHAT SMELLS and it was me.

At this point, I'm willing to hose down their clothes in friggin' napalm if I thought it would cover up the smell of teen angst.

What happened to me? I used to read ingredient lists, hunting down the parabens and phthalates like some kind of chemical detective. I used to buy expensive organic snacks, avoid preservatives, and shop at farmers' markets. Now I shop online for the discount snack foods with the biggest, bulkiest clearance price and let the grocery people haul it out to my car while I keep the motor running with Metallica playing loudly to drown out the sound of my kids fighting. Because they eat like carrion birds, clearing carcasses in mere minutes, and the tiny bags of organic bird seed don't last like they used to.

I started my parenting journey buoyed by high standards and a shocking display of optimism. Nothing but the best for my kid. I would choose the healthiest, most earth- and human-friendly products ever to grace the lips and wrinkly buttocks of a baby, and I would nail this parenting gig 100 percent.

My how the mighty have fallen. I don't know if I've lowered my standards or I've slowly succumbed to the relentlessness of parenting multiple kids and dealing with their onslaught of hormones, schedules, and gaping maws.

I look back on my carefully portioned ice cube trays of homemade baby food and chuckle ruefully and/or snort deridingly depending on my mood. Honestly? I wouldn't change a thing, then or now. I love the mom I started as. She cloth-diapered and composted and supplied her loved ones with the best of the best. And I love the mom I am now. I juggle one thousand balls in the air and somehow keep everyone fed, clothed, on time to sports practices, games, and meets, and smelling within the spectrum of socially acceptable. I have so much respect for both the moms I've been.

We gotta do what works for us in whatever stage we're in, and we can't take crap from anyone about it, especially from our former selves. Whether you're an all-natural, organic-loving parent or chucking store-brand crackers at your kids in the backseat of the minivan, or like me, a little bit of both, big ol' fist bump. We're killing it, and by it, I mean the smell.

Your Body's Gonna Go Through Some Changes

Puberty is a swear word in our house. If I want to freak out my kids, I just start chanting "pubertypubertypuberty" over and over. If I asked you to think back to when you were a kid and went through puberty, some stories probably come to mind. Maybe you were a late bloomer, and it felt like everyone had boobs but you. Maybe you were dying to get your period, then when it finally happened you wished you could give it back. I don't know guy stuff, but based on my expansive knowledge of sitcoms, it seems like a lot of surprise boners and trying to think about Grandma, Bob Ross, or anyone to make your happy tree go away.

I was an early bloomer, and it was embarrassing being one of like two girls with boobs in the third grade. In fourth grade one of the boys asked if he could milk me, so I think everyone was weirded out about what was happening on my chest, including me. Growing up is awkward.

People ask me which is harder—big kids or little kids?—but really both kinds are hard. I like big kids better. Onward and upward.

When it comes to everything happening to our kids as they grow up, my advice is strap in and don't get weird. Have open conversations. Don't flinch and don't act embarrassed. Look them in the eye, relax your face, and say the thing. It's not shameful or weird, it's normal and natural, so stay calm.

I had the basic puberty "this is what happens to your body" talk before fifth grade with two of my kids, and earlier with my youngest because youngest kids are just exposed to everything sooner. The timing depends on your kid.

It's pretty much biology. I included sex in the discussion,

but only from a biological "this is how babies are made and why your uterus sloughs itself once a month" standpoint, not any of the dating and rounding the bases stuff. That came a year later. (See chapter 14 for more details about that.) I talked about the mechanics, anatomy, and design of everything, and they asked follow-up questions.

People make these conversations into a big deal, but they really, really aren't. Whenever one of my kids makes an observation about new body development, my standard reaction is, "Yep, it happens." Pretty much every human since the dawn of time has gone through it, so I'm pretty sure we'll survive, too.

One time my kid asked what tampons were, and I just offhandedly mentioned how when women are older, they use them once a month, and that was enough of an answer at that time. About a year later, she had more questions about periods, and I mentioned about the bleeding. I explained how pregnancy works, and she immediately stuffed a balloon up her shirt, pretended to breathe through contractions, and delivered the balloon baby in the middle of the kitchen. All while I was peeling carrots for dinner. Don't even worry about it. You'll be fine.

When Am I Allowed to . . . ?

We have a five-year spread between our three kids. Some people have an even bigger age range, maybe because they have more kids or had a ten-year dry spell then a surprise from a faulty IUD. Whatever, I don't know your life. Maybe you only have one kid or two back-to-back. Our five-year range can feel gargantuan when they hit certain milestones.

The gap gets tricky when it comes to activities, and the little one has seen movies I wouldn't have dreamed of letting the older ones see when they were her age. Youngest kids have all the fun, but they never appreciate it because they have chips on their shoulders watching the big kids do things they can't.

I usually let her tag along, but sometimes even I can't stomach an eight- or nine-year-old seeing a certain movie that I deem fine for the older ones. And sometimes my youngest can't handle sitting still in a restaurant that my oldest would appreciate.

So, we've instituted Big Kid Night around here. The majority of my time is spent with my youngest, who, being the youngest, needs me a lot more, so I feel zero guilt about leaving her with a cool babysitter or letting her have a sleepover with Grammy and Granddaddy while Alex and I take the two older kids out for dinner and a movie.

This last time, within minutes of getting in the car, we'd covered sex, virginity, underage drinking, and swearing. They manage to lock down the questions around baby sis, but when they get a chance to hang out with just us, they let things fly, and we have some great conversations.

I don't know about you, but dropping a kid also changes the dynamic. There's less fighting, and everything feels shiny and reasonable. It's delightful. When we had two kids originally, it was overwhelming, but adding a third ramped it up exponentially, so now when we have only two it feels easy. If you have four kids and drop to three now and then, you probably know what I mean. It's fun getting to focus on a smaller group now and then.

If going out in public with your children makes you want to drive your van off a bridge, try taking one or two at a time and rotating it. If a sitter or family member isn't an option, swap with a friend. She can watch the littles while you take the bigs and then switch.

When it comes to the privileges and responsibilities that come with age, I try to have lots of conversations rather than hard-and-fast rules. As with most things, we start with a little responsibility and work our way up.

With babysitting, we started by putting Ana in charge and going out for coffee down the street for an hour. No one died, so we did that a few more times before working up to a two-hour dinner down the street. Then we went a little farther down the street. We paid her to babysit, and we gave our other kids a dollar each as incentive to behave.

When they want to do things with their friends, we take it on a case-by-case basis. We don't say, "This is what we did for your sibling; therefore, this is what we'll do for you." Our kids are very different, so we make decisions for each of them separately.

When Ana wanted to start wearing makeup, here's what we did. It's not a formula, but feel free to use this and adapt it to your unique situation and child. In sixth grade, Ana really wanted to start wearing makeup. I said no. She joined a makeup club at school and came home every Wednesday looking like Tammy Faye Bakker went goth. I created a hygiene checklist as a pathway to makeup and told her that if she incorporated everything on the list into her regular routine, without me having to remind her all the time, then she'd get makeup for seventh grade. Makeup has to start with a clean face, or it will just add to the problems. On the list:

Brush teeth, morning and night
Wash face, morning and night

Brush hair
Shower
Shave
Deodorant

At a weekend away, just me and her, during the summer before seventh grade, we talked about dating and sex, friendships and all the growing-up stuff, and at the end, I presented her with a makeup bag filled with makeup and brushes. I told her to start with the things in the bag and develop a solid routine, and then in eighth grade I'd let her add in more items.

I told her she'd be responsible for buying her own makeup after this, so as a responsible teen, she'd need to do chores, get babysitting jobs, and figure out how to pay for it. I love giving her this responsibility because instead of whining for me to buy her everything, she goes to the store, price compares all the options, and figures out what's in her budget, what she can do without, and what she wants to ask for before Christmas and her birthday. In the bag:

Mascara
Translucent powder
Concealer
Eyeshadow palette
Blush
Colored lip gloss

After spending a year perfecting her technique with the first batch, in eighth grade I finally let her add eyeliner, brow filler, and good grief, I have no idea. She's surpassed my rudimentary knowledge of makeup at this point. Maybe your kid isn't even into makeup, and this isn't a thing in your house. Cool. If your daughter is like mine, and makeup is an outlet for creative expression, this is what we did, and it's worked for us.

When my daughter turned thirteen, I asked the women in her life, relatives, neighbors, and mentors from our church, to write her letters, and I put them together in a book. We had a party for her, and each woman went around the circle and read her letter out loud to Ana. Ana was concerned this was her only party. A party with old people? I assured her she'd still have a pool party with her friends. This was a bonus party. Even though it was a little awkward for her, it meant a lot, and I loved seeing the women who loved Ana assembled around her. I told her these people were here for her through the teen years and beyond. She could turn to any one of them when she had a problem, if there was something she was afraid to talk to me about.

They're going to need more than you. That may be hard to hear, but ask yourself this: did you tell your parents everything when you were a teenager? I want my kids surrounded by trusted adults, people they think are cooler than me, people I've vetted and carefully moved into place.

I got to be that trusted adult for other people's kids. Starting with a group of sixth-graders at our church, Alex hung out with the boys, and I hung out with the girls. We met with them every week, fielded late-night texts, navigated friend drama, and listened while they tried to figure out their lives for seven years, until they graduated. They taught me so much, and now that I have big kids of my own, it's not as scary because I've been here before with other people's teens.

How to Talk to a Big Kid

Twelve-year-old girls are the worst. I adore my teen daughter with every fiber of my being, but when she was twelve, I was pretty sure she was demon-possessed. Your only options are to wait it out or call a priest.

Raising daughters for me is like, "I want to kill her with my bare hands she is waging emotional warfare and one of us will not survive this—oh my gosh! I love her so much can't wait to talk to her, we have so much funnnn!"

The way I talk to my kids has changed as they've gotten older. For one thing, I'm trying to delete the word *potty* from my vocabulary, but it's an uphill battle. I'm also trying to stop referring to myself in the third person. "Mommy thinks your SAT scores are wonderful" sounds ridiculous. And I'm trying to stop calling Alex Daddy, because when your kids are little, it's cute, but when they're older it's just creepy and weird and I don't want to be that sixty-year-old empty nester still calling her partner Daddy.

The other day one of my kids laughed and said, "Remember when you wouldn't let us say *heck*?" Yes, the good old days when the f-word was *fart* and no one would snort when I lost my dryer balls and ran around the house yelling, "Has anyone seen my balls?"

As they run out the door for school in the morning, I find myself yelling things like, "JESUS LOVES YOU VAPING IS BAD!" The way I talk to my kids has changed, and the way they talk to me has changed, too.

The older they get, the later they want to stay up and talk. The older I get, the earlier I want to go to bed. So, it's a challenge. In

213

those quiet moments when you're able to hang out, here are some ways to approach them.

First, ask questions. Ask questions ask questions ask questions. So often we want to start lecturing or talking a mile a minute at them. Pause, breathe, ask, and wait. Start with easy ones if they freeze up. Like a lie detector test. Is your name Ana Dale? Do you live in Georgia? Then find the right questions to unlock your child.

Approach your kids with unconditional respect. I try to use this one in all my relationships. We talk a lot about unconditional love, and I tell my kids, "I love you all the time, no matter what." That's important. But equally important is respect. I crave respect from the people who matter most to me, so I want to be generous with it to my kids. If their actions cause me to lose trust for them in an area, I always want them to know they have my respect, and they can gain back my trust. Even when a kid is acting in a way that's hard to respect, I look for places, even small ones, where I can show respect. "I see how you started to talk back to me and then redirected. I respect that self-control." Look for ways to tell them you respect the way they treat their friends or organize their time or talk to adults or get ready for school. Tell them you respect them as often as you can, as often as you tell them you love them.

Affirm their skills and good choices. We have a habit in this society of bad-mouthing teens. We joke about teens being bad drivers, or lazy, or stupid. As parents, we have the opportunity to affirm our kids amidst a sea of negativity. When my kids first got behind the wheel of the golf cart (in our community, twelve-year-olds can drive golf carts with adult supervision), they were nervous, and I kept saying, "You're going to be a great driver. I can tell you're careful and cautious." Were my butt cheeks clenched to their full capacity? You betcha. But my kids needed to hear that they could do this. "Thanks for coming home right on time. You're great at respecting my curfew." "Your creativity really makes you awesome at school projects." "You're good at supporting your friends. You're such a good friend to have." Even if they roll their eyes or say something snarky back, affirm your big kids whenever you can.

Our greatest strength as a family is our humor. For all the positive stuff I just said, our wit and snappy comebacks make it all go down without gagging. We are not precious people, and if we had to just be nice and gooey all the time we'd die. Whether we're laughing and having fun, or arguing like it's our family's varsity sport, we lace it all with a hearty dose of inappropriate, uproarious humor. Laugh with your kids, laugh at your kids, and let them laugh at you. Seriously, don't take things too seriously. Even the serious stuff. When our kids think their world is falling apart and their vision tunnels down to that one moment and everything feels impossible, we validate their feelings, give them solid ground in the storm, and then when they're ready, offer them our greatest gift: perspective. We know that life will go on, that they will survive this hard thing, and we can teach them to laugh in the face of it. Laughter makes us brave.

Don't freak out when they tell you stuff, because it'll shut them down and you want them to talk. Teens are like ketchup bottles. You open them and hold them upside down and wait for what feels like ages. You give them a little tap now and then to speed up the process. Then finally, they start to spill. Slowly, just a bit. If you hold the bottle just right, you'll get all the ketchup you need. So, don't overreact and scare the ketchup. No matter what they tell you. Don't freak. Freak out with a friend or your partner right after, but in that moment, stay calm. Unless a random saying starts to become a refrain. "Ugh, I wanna kill myself" is teen for "A friend didn't text me back within three seconds." But if it becomes a refrain, check in with them and see what's going on and make sure they're okay and call the therapist.

The Balance Between Being a Safe Place and Scaring the Shpoo Out of Them

One of my favorite things about having big kids is the movies get better. My kids are old enough that we get to introduce them to movies we love, and there's nothing more endearing than hearing your children quote *The Princess Bride* at the dinner table. They're even starting to get into scary movies, which warms my adrenaline-loving sicko heart.

Our community hosts "dive-in" movie nights throughout the summer, where the kids can eat popcorn, swim, and watch movies on a big blow-up screen at the edge of the pool. Last summer, they showed the movie *Jaws*, and I excitedly took my kids to see this beloved classic. My children, while swimming in the pool in the dark, would get to watch a killer shark eat people. Partway through, after the jump scare with the underwater dead guy, my two youngest sidled over to me, dripping wet. Elliott, a direct man who knows what he wants, said, "I'll never get that picture out of my head. Take me home now." (This year, a switch flipped for Elliott and he wants all the scary things.) Evie, a little more cunning and unwilling to admit defeat, said, "I'm not scared. I'm not, Mom. I'm just ANGRY. I'm angry that people keep dying, so I want to go home, too. Because I'm angry not scared." Ana was happily teenagering with her friends in an oversized inner tube. Nothing goes better with the teen years than classic horror flicks.

Parenting is a balance between providing a safe place to land and serving up enough fear to keep your kids alive and engaged. Okay, maybe killer sharks aren't always the best choice, but a healthy dose of scare tactics may keep our kids on the right track.

No one was better at providing a loving, nurturing home while simultaneously scaring me into a full colon cleanse than my mother. As a teen, I was on High Alert for all the dangers that could befall me. It's actually really impressive, considering I grew up before the internet was a thing, and Mom had to actually scour newspapers and watch hours of news for horrible things to warn me about.

Every morning at breakfast she'd pile newspaper clippings of the latest rapes and abductions. Before I went to college, she made me read *Not Without My Daughter* to make sure I properly vetted any boyfriends.

When I started driving, that's when Mom really began to shine. Every time I'd sit behind the wheel of our silver Taurus wagon, I'd place my hands at ten and two and she'd intone, "Now remember, you're in a Death Machine." Got it, Mom. And in that spirit, I set forth.

Now that I'm a parent, I find myself trying to strike a balance between safety and terror. "Nothing bad is going to happen, UNLESS YOU SHARE PERSONAL INFORMATION ONLINE. Then a stranger's going to show up at our house, break into your room, steal your iPhone, and post photos of you drooling on yourself asleep." "You are completely safe, UNLESS YOU BREAK CURFEW. Then you'll be murdered on the way home, and your killer will wear your intestines like a statement necklace."

Before my girls graduate, I'm definitely making them watch *Taken*, and at the end I'm going to look them in the eye and say, "Your parents . . . do not have a particular set of skills. Unless you're abducted by someone willing to swap you for a new logo or some light editorial work, no one is coming to rescue you."

10 WAYS TO DEFUSE A TEEN BOMB (PROCEED WITH CAUTION)

1. Hand them chocolate.
2. Write them an encouraging note and stick it to their mirror or in their bag.
3. Pray a blessing over them while driving and they can't fling themselves out of the car.
4. Look for an opportunity to affirm their decision about something.
5. Show them respect.
6. Keep lectures short.
7. Ask them specific, rather than general questions. Start with easy ones.
8. Run a bubble bath.
9. Surprise them with little treats.
10. Invite them to grab a coffee or milkshake.

13

I Hope I Still Like You After They're Gone

Lighten Up About Marriage

"No, thanks. I already had a wife."
—*From Dusk Till Dawn*

I know not every parent is married or in a committed partnership, and if that's you, feel free to skip this chapter. But a lot of parents are, so I thought I'd spend one chapter talking about it, because for those of us who are, we're hoping to still be happy about it after the kids move out. I mean, that's probably the goal.

And if you were married and aren't anymore, I'm sorry or congratulations, depending on how that all went down. Marriage is hard, and sometimes it doesn't work out, and sometimes you need to get out of it to save yourself and your kids. No judgment here. I don't know your circumstances. But for those of us still together and trying to keep it that way, for those of us with partners willing to chip in and help with that, this chapter is for us.

Parenting can be hard on a relationship. I'm not supposed to say that. But it is. We've had professionals and friends tell us over and over about the divorce rate for parents of kids with special needs.[14] They kept warning us to stay vigilant! Work on your marriage! Thanks, everyone. No pressure. No matter what you're juggling with your kids, the truth is your relationship can get wrapped up in parenting and you can lose a sense of what brought you together in the first place. We've found that a combination of regular time together without the kids and spending plenty of time laughing AT our kids helps keep our marriage relatively strong.

Your New Favorite Pastime: Laughing at Your Kids

Alex and I tied the knot back in the year 2000, and if you ask me how we keep our relationship healthy after all these years, I feel like I should talk about date nights and communication, but really, we laugh at our kids behind their backs a lot.

That's what my parents did to me (still do to me), and they've been married for forty-some years. I'd sashay into the room and spout off whatever fascinating opinion I'd developed after copious research, dazzle myself with my own logical reasoning, and the edges of their mouths would twitch. I assumed it was because they were impressed as I dismantled their inferior way of thinking and

---

14 This article refutes this concern and presents reason to hope from the fifty-year Wisconsin Longitudinal Study, published by the NIH; Calleen Petersen, "Are Divorce Rates Really Higher for Parents of Kids with Disabilities?" *The Mighty*, March 23, 2018. https://themighty.com/2018/03/divorce-rates-parents-of-kids-with -disabilities/.

they embraced my insight, but I now know that as soon as my teen booty cleared the doorframe on my way out, they dissolved into a puddle of laughter.

That's what we do now. (If you're reading this, honey, I don't mean you. I mean your siblings. Of course. Whichever one of you is reading this right now, you were wise and knowledgeable about all things, and we respected your mature thought process.)

You will not survive parenting kids unless you learn to laugh at them, and I don't mean laugh with them. Laugh at them. Wait till after they leave the room. We're not monsters (maybe a little).

One of the best ways to bring you and your partner together is to spend time enjoying how ridiculous your offspring are. They are utterly ridiculous. Small humans are wildly entertaining, and you'll do well to lighten up a bit about what they're saying and find the funny.

Every day my kids impart some new revelation or life goal, and we've learned not to take every statement seriously. Don't take it seriously, unless they repeat it a lot. "You're going to start a You-Tube channel, amass wealth, move into your own mansion, and never talk to us again? Tell us more about this exciting new endeavor." When one of our kids went off about our gross minivan and how they were going to drive a Lambo someday, we nearly died laughing, after translating Lambo into our sad, middle-class vernacular. We advised this kid to work hard in school if they saw a Lamborghini in their future, but I think they're just going with the YouTube plan.

Alex and I spend hours together laughing about our kids. On Saturday mornings, we sequester ourselves on the enclosed porch with the dogs and our coffee while the kids press themselves against the glass door trying to get in. Whenever things start looking grim around here, I can always count on a good gut laugh to clear the air. It may be end-of-days, apocalyptic humor, "Bahahahaa it's all going down in flames!" but at least we're laughing together.

It Doesn't Have to Be Magical All the Time

I struggle in the romance department. I've never watched the Hallmark Channel, although with a teen girl in the house I'm thinking about trying the age-old bonding ritual of mother-daughter rom-com watching. I texted my mother, who's loved Hallmark movies since before they were cool, for suggestions on a good one with a cute boy in it who Ana would like, and she immediately texted me back about one starring Henry Winkler.

What? No, Mom, no. Henry Winkler is not attractive to a teen girl. I'm thinking someone younger. She clarified that The Fonz plays the uncle in the movie and sent a photo of the "cute young man" who stars in it. He looks like he's my age, which is old.

I wrote back, "Nevermind I can't do this," and a barfy face emoji. I can't do Hallmark movies. The only one I want to see is starring Jason Momoa, called *Where Did Santa's Shirt Go?* and they spend the whole movie looking for it, then at the end they decide he doesn't need it because he has his Christmas spirit to keep him warm.

But I can't tell anyone that, because I've reached the age when my being sexually attracted to someone is considered abhorrent to the general population. Middle-aged moms are supposed to pour all their icky sexual urges into chocolate chip cookies, but I don't bake. One day I was watching TV with Ana when the trailer for *Aquaman* came on. She and I watched in silence, and then in unison breathed, "He is so hot," and her head whipped toward me and she chastised, "Mom! You're married to Dad! Ew!" And I answered, "It's not like he's coming to live with us. I'm looking at Aquaman in his little Spandex-y pants saying, 'Good job with that one, God! Nice work!'" And she tried to keep down the Nutella she'd just eaten as the air around her smelled of putrid, thirsty old lady.

I can't handle gooey romance, but Alex has found other ways to show me love, like how he knocked it out of the park on a recent birthday, with a late night, *IT*-themed birthday surprise. The night before my birthday, I was at a friend's house watching horror movies until late. Before I got home, Alex texted that he was tired and heading to bed. I walked into a dark house and tiptoed up the stairs, where I saw a lone red balloon tied to a paper boat. I chuckled to myself, murmuring "niiice" under my breath, and quietly opened my bedroom door so I wouldn't wake anybody up. I was greeted by red flickering light and a talking clown, and as my eyes adjusted to the dark, I realized the entire room was covered in red balloons tied to paper boats, and instead of SS *Georgie*, the boats said SS *Melanie*. I started laughing with delight, and as I twirled around in my very own birthday horror surprise, my kids and darling husband jumped out to hug me. Some men sprinkle the bed with rose petals. My guy knows the way to my heart.

After all these years, I can tell you that I still love him. I still love him, but my understanding of love has dramatically changed over the last couple decades. When I was young, love was a feeling I had in my heart, and sometimes lower. That feeling was ooey-gooey and came with pet names and concern that I might die if our skin didn't touch. These days, after wrangling kids all day long, I feel like I might die if our skin does touch. Please give me a two-foot buffer at all times, partner.

I love him, but I love him away. I love him over there, across the room. Calm the heck down about romance. Your marriage doesn't have to be gooey to be good.

Your Marriage Doesn't Have to Look Like Anyone Else's

In a world that idolizes romantic love, I would like to spend a little ink in defense of pragmatic love. After all, we don't all have the same personality, so why should our love look the same?

We don't have a gooey relationship, but we have a well-maintained one, and that's what's important to me. If you're raising kids with a partner, is your relationship well-maintained? Are you putting in the work to keep it healthy? I don't need a fancy marriage, but I do want a healthy one, and our partnership doesn't have to look like anyone else's.

A few years ago, Alex and I stopped sleeping together. We still badonkadonk, but we don't sleep in the same bed when we're done, because between his sleep apnea and my light sleeper–nea we were angry at each other all the time. He'd snore, I'd passive aggressively sigh, he'd snore louder, I'd plain ol' aggressively kick him in the solar plexus, and so on and so forth for an eternity of marriage. We realized we were basing our marriage on that of our parents, friends, and random rom-coms we'd seen where loving couples spoon all night in a sweaty embrace.

Spooning all night makes me feel like I'm in a hostage situation. I'm stuck in a headlock and can't breathe, and now my captor is snoring in my ear full throttle. What kind of cruel and unusual punishment is this? In addition to being taken prisoner I have to be subjected to noise torture, too? This kind of torture belongs in the Tower of London of yore along with the Rack and Scavenger's Daughter.

So, we sleep on entirely different floors of the house and we like it that way. That's just one example of the many ways we've had to lighten up about having a marriage that looks like those of our parents and the people around us. It's okay to be different and do things that work for your own unique relationship. The important thing is to find what works, for the sake of your children as well as your sanity. With our sleeping arrangement, it would be too easy never to interact, so we make sure to check a lot of boxes in the "quality time" department. (So romantic, right? Checking boxes. Ooh baby. I can feel it in my tiny, shriveled Grinch heart.)

Every Friday morning, we go for breakfast and reconnect over coffee and bacon. Somewhere in year two of our marriage a pastor at our church gave us two questions to ask each other, and we've been asking these same two questions every week since.

1. How have you felt loved by me this week?
2. How can I love you better?

I like these questions because over the years we've learned how each of us experiences love, not how we think the other person should feel loved. Alex feels love when I make him a sandwich or bring him a cup of coffee. He could make me one thousand sandwiches and I'll appreciate it, but I won't feel loved until he sits down with me while I eat it and has a conversation, preferably while playing with my hair. And then the second question keeps us from building up too much junk before resolving any tension that's crept in. Maybe one of us is doing something that's rubbing the other one the wrong way. Maybe a big thing happened, and we need to talk through it and apologize and forgive. I do my best apologizing and growing as a person over coffee and bacon.

Recently, I told Alex we need to have scheduled sex nights, because with our kids grown up and never going to bed and us at various sporty practices and running an unpaid Uber service at all hours, we let too much time go between naked time, and pretty soon we're just really good housemates. I approached him apologetically about needing to schedule sex, but I think all he heard was sex, and that he could count on having more of it, so he was on board with the plan, no matter how unromantic it sounded.

So now, in addition to our Friday morning breakfast routine, we have scheduled sex nights. I won't tell you which nights because I don't want you thinking about us doing it. (And there may be unscheduled sex as well, but there's at least the standing commitments. I mean, not that we're standing. That sounds exhausting. You know what? Mind your own business.)

Sex night is especially helpful because we both know going into it that we need to get our crap together, get the kids upstairs, finish up work, and get our heads in the game. (That may or may not be a penis joke. You decide. More about sex in the next chapter.)

In addition to the weekly breakfast date, we also have a monthly date in downtown Atlanta. For a few years we went in with another couple on season tickets to the theater, and paying in advance kept us committed to showing up monthly and having a great night together in nice clothes. We had a schedule of shows a year out so we could plan and prioritize. Maybe you hate theater, and it could be sports or movies or reservations to new restaurants. Whatever it is, put date nights on the calendar and stick to them to the best of your ability.

Most of our time together isn't fancy and expensive. Probably our favorite thing is just watching a crap ton of Netflix together and quoting movie lines.

Your relationship with your partner doesn't have to be magical all the time. If it is, awesome, and you're probably wired that way, with lovely, healthy feelings and emotions. Buy flowers and be romantic and post it all on Facebook so the rest of us can ogle it.

But if you're like me, pragmatic and unromantic, you can still have a fantastic relationship with your partner. We communicate well. We spend regularly scheduled quality time together. And we have a pact. Whoever wants to leave first has to take the kids.

So, we both stick around, because neither one of us wants to do this alone. It's not perfect. We both have strong personalities and each think that we know what's best, but ultimately, we respect each other. We're committed to raising these young creatures together for the continuation of the human race and, hopefully, enjoying ourselves a little during the process.

The book of Ecclesiastes says, "Two are better than one, because they have a good return for their labor: If either of them falls down, one can help the other up. But pity anyone who falls and has no one to help them up." We help each other up. Of course, the next verse says, "Also, if two lie down together, they will keep warm. But how can one keep warm alone?"[15] I find two comforters, a heating pad, and a scrappy Maltipoo named Khaleesi do the trick.

I'm thankful to have a partner who wants to do the work,

---

15 Ecclesiastes 4:9–11 (NIV).

someone who's reasonable and dependable and a good friend and solid guy. I know not everyone has someone like that, so I'm not trying to tell you to be like us. If things got toxic and you needed to leave, all you'll get from me is a hug and an offer to watch your kids if you need a night out. (Although after reading this book you might not want to leave them with me. Your call.)

Ideally, we work hard while raising the kids so that once we launch them out into the world, we like each other enough that we want to carry on. I mean, that's the dream, right? I remember when my brother and I went to college, my parents started doing all this stuff. They went to Sam's Club on Friday nights and ate free samples together. Their social calendar filled up, and I started noticing they weren't around to take my phone calls. Had we been holding them back? Were they super-fun people all these years and we just couldn't tell because they were too busy driving us to all our stuff and grounding us for missing curfew? After spending two decades of their life together raising my brother, Nate, and me, they were still BFFs and loved being together. Hashtag squad goals.

I decided I wanted the same thing, so even though we're smack in the middle of Crazytown with the kids, by scheduling time together and working on strong communication and finding ways to keep the fun in our relationship, I hope that in another decade when our last kid flies away, Alex and I will still want to hang.

Fight in Front of the Kids, Make Up in Front of the Kids

Alex and I argue a lot. I already told you we're yellers. We are just naturally loud, opinionated tyrants who think we're right and are ready to throw down at a moment's notice. As long as we're both breathing, I don't see that changing. Two things save us: communication and humility. We have to work hard at both.

We have some established ground rules for fighting, and these have helped us navigate through a couple decades' worth of conflict.

We fight fairly. When we're arguing, we don't blast each other where it hurts, and we don't use a fight as an opportunity to dig into an old wound or sensitive area. We try not to throw around words we can't take back. We don't call each other names or be mean to each other. I like winning arguments, but I don't like destroying my partner in the process.

We don't always hide our disagreements from the kids either. Sometimes, depending on the subject matter, we take it behind closed doors, but if it's an acceptable subject, we're willing to disagree in front of the kids. But if we start a fight in front of them, we finish in front of them, too. We want them to see that disagreement is healthy and normal, and this is how we work through it and resolve our differences in a productive way. My kids will try to get involved, crowing things like, "Ooh, Mommm, nice burn!" And I have to shut that shoot right down. "Oh, you think you're all grown and a part of this? Quiet down and let the grown-ups talk." We are not "burning" each other. We are having an argument, and we will resolve it. This is healthy.

I don't want my kids to think their parents' marriage was this magical unicorn that just happened. Yes, we're lucky and blessed and whatever word you use to convey "so dang grateful it worked out for us." But we also work really, really hard to keep this ship seaworthy, and I want to model that work so if they get married someday, they won't panic if they hit a rough spot. I watched my parents argue and work through things, and I watched them kiss in the kitchen and dance around the living room. My kids see the same thing, to their utter consternation. Parents kissing is the most disgusting thing ever. When they were little, they'd try to wriggle between us, and now that they're older they make pukey noises till we stop.

Sometimes our kids try to use us against each other to get what they want. They stick a chisel in between us and try to pry us apart. Nope. Don't let them triangulate you. We are quick to tell our kids, "Daddy and I are on the same team." And then we huddle up privately to unravel whatever's going on. Our kids know that if we catch them trying to use one of us against the other, they'll get in more trouble than if they'd just faced us to begin with. So much of parenting together is figuring out what's going on, getting on the same page with your partner, then presenting a united front.

If at any point communication fails, or if we can't reach an agreement, or hurt each other in the process, then humility is important. Over the years we've had to learn how to be wrong. We've both had lots of practice at this. We get things wrong so often, but as you learn to admit it and ask forgiveness, it gets easier. Humility gets easier the more you practice it, even for those of us jackholes to whom it does not come naturally.

I spend so much time managing our kids' stuff that I consider myself an expert. I am the foremost expert on our children, which makes it hard for me when Alex has a different opinion about parenting. How dare he weigh in? I've read more articles, talked with more parents, and attended more doctor appointments, therapy sessions, and teacher conferences than he has. I want him to sign off on all my decisions without question. However. They are his kids, too, and he often has insights and suggestions that I need to hear. So, I'm learning to hear his opinions. And he's learning to respect my expertise and the work that I do. Over the years, our communication has gotten stronger in the face of bigger and more life-altering challenges. Mutual respect is everything.

My kids like to ask me who's my favorite, and they bat their eyes and look as adorable as possible, but my answer stays the same. Their dad. Alex is my favorite.

10 TIPS FOR PARTNERING WHILE PARENTING

1. Schedule weekly one-on-one time to talk.
2. Balance talking about the kids with talking about each other.
3. Laugh at the kids together.
4. Fight fairly.
5. Learn how to be wrong.
6. Your relationship doesn't have to look like anyone else's.
7. Healthy maintenance is better than gooey feelings.
8. Stay on the same team.
9. Prioritize time together without the kids.
10. Practice mutual respect.

14

"Mom, You Only Had Sex the One Time, Right?"

Lighten Up About Sex

"It rubs the lotion on its skin."
—*The Silence of the Lambs*

Right when I was starting to enjoy sex, my kids grew up and we had to start talking to them about it. I tell myself over and over again, "Don't make it weird, Melanie." Kids have a natural desire to ask questions about their bodies, babies, and dating, and if we don't make it weird, they won't either, at least until they hit about middle school, and then everything is weird 100 percent of the time.

When the kids are little, your body is a battered, exhausted bounce house. The kids ride you, yank you, and smear stuff on you all day. Sometimes I was so tired I let my son bury me in the couch and jump on me just for a chance to lie down. So, finding the energy for sex is hard. You're really tired, and you wish you could just give your partner permission to do you while you're asleep. When the kids get older, your body becomes yours again, but instead of finding the energy, you have trouble finding the time. They are always awake trying to talk to you. They know everything that happens in the house. You feel like horny teenagers trying to find a dark corner. You find yourselves scheduling it between swim team and lacrosse practice and wondering if you can just start ahead of time and hope he jumps in before it's over.

As your kids get older, you have to start talking with them about their own sexy stuff, which will hopefully be happening way, way in the future. It'll be fine. Don't freak out and they won't freak out. I actually really enjoy these conversations, and it doesn't have to be terrifying.

"Go Away So I Can Bang Your Dad," and Other Things You Wish You Could Say

I'm going to talk about us having the sex before I cover talking with our kids about it, because as you already know, once they enter the picture it gets awkward and there's no going back from that.

We didn't have a lot of sex while I was pregnant, because, first, I was a little nervous after all the in vitro and stuff we did to help make him, and then because I was super sick with preeclampsia and so on and so forth. After I had Elliott, I thought we'd get back to the sexing eventually. The doctor said six weeks, but I had a C-section and contemplated telling Alex six months instead. Everything hurt, and nursing made it weird. I wondered, *But what*

234

about my nipples? Sex while breastfeeding was confusing. All the men in my life needed a piece of me, and I felt hunted. I wished our species was into hibernation.

"Everything is leaking, and I need a minute!"

After our long battle with infertility, producing a child and deciding to pursue adoption took the pressure off our long-suffering pistil and stamen and reawakened the joy of sex, and eventually we more or less got into the swing of things. And then the kids got older and sex became a game of whether or not we could stay awake long enough to do it.

As the kids get older, you get your body back and no longer need to nurse, carry, or wipe anyone, the triumvirate of lady boner killers. You start to think you might enjoy some of the sex again. But right when you pour that glass of wine and head to bone town, your kids assault you with homework questions, text you for a pickup from late-night lacrosse practice, or want to watch *Saturday Night Live* with you. What. Why are they still awake? And why do they want to interact with you? And why can't they still have a 7:00 p.m. bedtime?

If you're going to maintain some semblance of a sex life with children under your roof, you have to lighten up about sex. It might not look like it does in the movies. You might hide lingerie under your college sweatshirt, so the kids won't see. Prioritize togetherness over perfection. The perfect foreplay culminating in simultaneous orgasms might not happen after chucking the kids in their rooms, cleaning the kitchen, packing lunches, and feeding the dogs.

We had to start doing it in the basement because our kids are up at all hours of the night. During the day, when I'm reminding them about math problems or calling them to dinner, they can't hear me, but at night they're like bats with sonar and sense every little bump and crackle, whether it's the wrapper from my emergency chocolate stash or me trying to bang their dad. So, we skulk like horny teenagers to the basement, lock the door, and hope for the best.

We told our daughter about the basement sex, and now if we need her to get gone, we just mention that we're going to the basement, she makes a gagging noise, and runs upstairs. This is great and frees us up to watch *Game of Thrones* uninterrupted.

Talking to Your Kids About the Sex

At some point we have to talk with our kids about sex. Stay calm. The most important thing is to jump in and talk to them yourself, so they don't have to be the wide-eyed kids at school hearing everything for the first time from their teacher in a room full of glandular preteens. Don't make them experience that. By the time school does its thing, you want to equip your kids with enough information that they aren't blindsided. The earlier you start, the more likely they'll actually be curious and secretly want to know stuff. Once they've learned it elsewhere, they go back to thinking you're a doofus. I tell my kids that their dad and I have been doing it for a long time, so we're basically sex experts.

The mistake parents make is thinking there is one Big Talk that needs to happen. It's actually more of a series of talks. I told my kids this is the beginning of a lifelong conversation. You don't just have one talk and then leave them to it. You have layer upon layer of conversations.

Biology

The first talk we had covered basic biology. Which holes are where and what they are for. How babies are made, unless you're Elliott, in which case you were made with a turkey baster and a test tube. Our school shows the kids a video in fifth grade so for us, we started these conversations well before that, because we wanted to be the ones to kick it off.

Dating and Marriage

When they each turned twelve, we took the kids on a one-on-one weekend away, kind of a coming-of-age mother-daughter or father-son special retreat. On this weekend, in addition to fun stuff catered specifically to our individual kid's interests, we dealt with friendships, dating, and marriage stuff. We unpacked how to develop healthy relationships, our thoughts on dating, and what to expect down the road. Then we talked about sex and all the things people do together. The mechanics of all the different ways body parts interact. We answered all their very specific questions and made sure they knew the slang and proper terms. If my daughter has a boy say he wants to *blah blah blah* her, I want her to know exactly what *blah blah blah* is and how fast to run away from this boy. We shared our feelings about morals and when we believe things should happen. We talked about strategies for resisting pressure to engage in things too soon.

Walking in a crowded parking lot after church:

Ana: Guess what we talked about in church today?

Me: What?

Ana: SEX!

Me: Awesome, but tell me in the car 'cos some of these parents might not want their toddlers to know yet.

Ana: Everyone was so embarrassed, and I was like, why? We talk about this stuff at the dinner table.

Me: True story.

Like with just about everything, I think we need to lighten up about this area. I was raised in a purity culture that focused on a lot of shame when it came to sexuality, not from my parents but more just the culture around us. On the other hand, some people never received any guidance whatsoever in this area. So, Alex and I tried to hit a healthy medium here, sharing our feelings about sex, how our faith influences our choices, and also freedom from shame and a thousand reminders that no matter what our kids decide to do, we love them completely.

Consent and Consequences

The next layer I added was consent. No one is allowed to do anything to them without their consent. Well before my kids ever started dating, I wanted both my son and my daughters to understand that they don't owe anyone anything nor does anyone owe anything to them. In my regular prayer rotation for my kids is praying that they would have wisdom and not let anyone take advantage of them. That they'd show self-control and not let anyone pressure them or dupe them into doing anything they don't want to. I talked to them about setting boundaries, that no means no, and how it's important to respect yourself and others.

As they continue to grow up, we talk about various celebrities in the news and consequences they're facing because of assault and poor judgment. In addition to crime, we talk about protection, birth control, and the emotional and physical responsibilities and consequences of sex. Personally, I hope my children remain tender virgins until their wedding nights, when they inexplicably morph into sexual dynamos and have happy, healthy marriages, producing a plethora of grandbabies. But since I can't know what the future holds, I try to cover all the bases.

Every now and then, something occurs to me randomly, and I panic that I forgot to mention it. What if my kid gets into trouble simply because I forgot a lesson? This leads to awkward, random situations like the following:

> **Me**: If a boy has a big cold sore on the corner of his mouth, don't kiss him. It's herpes, and it's contagious. Don't kiss herpes or you'll have it and get cold sores for the rest of your life.
> **Her**: I'm leaving now.
> **Me**: Okay, have fun at school!

I'm not a doctor. No idea if this is true, but it seemed important then. Another day, I launched in with this totally normal subject:

> **Me**: Hey honey, random thought, if a boy asks for something called a "blow job," that's oral sex, and just know that you will get nothing out of that arrangement. That's best left

for a loving, reciprocal relationship like what Dad and I have, where two people are committed to loving and serving each other.

Her: Imma go die in a hole.

Me: If a boy says you have to do that or he'll leave you, you don't want him.

Her:

Me: Okay, have fun at the football game!

Life moments with Mom. I realize I have a limited amount of time to impart all my parental wisdom, and I also don't want to miss my window on anything. I'd hate to not say something, and then a week later, she learns the hard way and I could've prevented it simply by shouting it to her out the window while dropping her off at practice when the thought occurred to me.

This thinking is how I end up mentioning the most intimate subjects nonchalantly in passing. My kids have learned to just stare straight ahead until I'm finished and then walk away before I decide to say any more. These attacks of drive-by momming are unprovoked and unanticipated. You cannot prepare for them. They swoop down from the sky, and my kids have to wait me out, making limited eye contact. But it's my right as their mother to share these things, and I may save them from heartache and/or mouth sores.

10 TIPS FOR TALKING ABOUT SEX

1. Start early.
2. Start simply. If your seven-year-old daughter asks what a tampon is, tell her it's for women to use once a month when they aren't pregnant. You don't have to diagram the missionary position at this point.
3. Teach your kids that you're a knowledgeable resource for them.
4. Don't be judgy.
5. Resist the urge to flinch away. Practice your neutral face in the mirror.
6. Scream into a pillow by yourself later if you need to.
7. Nothing is off-limits to talk about.
8. Earn their trust and show them you are trustworthy.
9. If you have a moral code or a book of scriptures that guides your life, weave that into these talks. I regularly pull out the Bible and talk about how God created sex. Yes, it makes it even more awkward. Yes, I'll keep doing it.
10. You don't have to share every detail from your own life. You're the adult and can choose to keep some things private.

15

I Worry My Kids Will Be Satanists

Lighten Up About Belief

"The power of Christ compels you."
—*The Exorcist*

I've been putting off this chapter because my own faith feels a little tenuous and up in the air these days, and trying to parent my kids while having a spiritual midlife crisis is hard enough, much less writing about it. But I'm including a chapter on belief in this book because even though we might be from different faith backgrounds or practice faith differently, many of us do consider faith a component of our lives, even if the size of that component varies for everyone. And even if you're an atheist, that's a belief system you're passing on to your kids as well, so we're all just trying to figure out how to parent through the lenses of our various beliefs.

I am a Christian, so my perspective is from that viewpoint. But the older I get, the more I try to use more inclusive language so that what I have to say can be applied to or considered by the wider world. I'll do my best, and if something doesn't apply to you, feel free to skip or ignore. Regardless of whether you believe like I do, I think we all want our kids to grow up to be kind, generous, loving, and faithful to something, and for a lot of us, religion can teach that.

Whether you're interested in passing up or passing on your belief system to your kids, I want us all to lighten up about the whole thing. I worry my kids will be Satanists, because I'm lucky if we actually pray before meals. (If you are a Satanist, maybe you totally pray before meals. I really don't know these things.) Most of us grew up with some kind of belief system, and when we become parents, we have to figure out if we want to pass it on to our kids, modify it, or disregard it altogether. Our decisions are compounded if we have partners who come from different backgrounds than ours. So many decisions. And not deciding is a decision.

I grew up in a pretty conservative though unconventional evangelical Christian family. My parents left the denomination of their youth when I was little and started a church in the basement of their friend's day-care center in Kentucky. I'd spend Sunday mornings working crossword puzzles, trying to ignore the preacher screaming at us. I don't think he was mad, just passionate, but I kept my head down and worked the crosswords all the same. That preacher may not have made me a Christian, but he sure as heck made me a nerd.

We moved from Kentucky to Northeastern Ohio when I was in kindergarten, and we hopped around awhile then eventually met for church in the apartment above my dad's vet clinic. When we sang hymns, the dogs in the kennels below would bark and howl along. Eventually, we started attending a local church that met in a warehouse, where attendees would take smoke breaks outside near the motorcycle parking and my Sunday school room was a glorified closet with the words "Hot Stick" painted on the door.

In a mostly Catholic town near Cleveland, and the only evangelical Christian I knew of in my school, I grew up feeling loved and super weird. My parents did their best to shelter me from all evil, raising me to "live in the world but not of it," whatever that meant. As a child of the 1980s, I knew it didn't mean "We Are the World," because that was a secular song, and those were not allowed in my childhood.

Sometime during my preteen years, I got my first CD player, and my dad took me to the Christian bookstore to pick out a CD. I made my way past the "Turn or Burn" tee-shirts and ruffled Bible covers to the wall of CDs. As the beginning of my brief dalliance with rap, I chose a CD featuring a group called J.C. & the Boyz, and after popping it into my new player, discovered an antidrug song called "Crack." Because J.C. was against it.

A couple years ago, while watching *The Tonight Show Starring Jimmy Fallon*, I listened to actor Matt Bomer tell virtually this exact story, down to the song about crack, and I felt so seen.[16] I was not the only one. I googled him and saw we were born two weeks apart and are both married with three kids. I'm wondering if I should watch his movie *Magic Mike*, just to be supportive of a fellow Christian bookstore patron.

Eventually, my parents either saw the light or gave up on me, and in 1989, more than one Iron Curtain was lifted. They let me start listening to rock music from the regular music store and I went straight for Guns N' Roses and Aerosmith and never looked back.

Now that I'm raising my own kids and trying to help them

---

16 *The Tonight Show Starring Jimmy Fallon*, https://www.nbc.com/the-tonight -show/video/matt-bomer-sings-his-fave-christian-rap-song-crack/3557891.

navigate the music world, maybe I've overcompensated. When Evie was six or seven, someone asked her what her favorite song was, and she said "Janie's Got a Gun."

Anyway, my parents were raised a way, tweaked it up when it was their turn, and I was raised a way, and now as a parent I'm figuring out what I want to keep and what I want to tweak. Maybe you can identify with that. Whether you were raised as a Christian, another religion, an atheist, or by conspiracy theorists in the back of a Winnebago, we all have to figure out what we want to do with the next generation.

Passing Up or Passing On Your Belief System to Your Kids

When I think about a belief system, I tend to think of religion, but your belief system encompasses more than that. For instance, in addition to Jesus, I'm drilling into my kids some pretty hardcore movie-watching beliefs. Two of my kids like to talk during movies and this does not fly in our family's culture, so I find myself hissing at them, "We do not talk in movies. Ever." Alex drolly intones, "Movies explain themselves," as they ask one million questions during the first scene. We are adamant about raising quiet movie-goers, but so far two of them are not embracing our belief system in this area, much to our chagrin.

In our family, we also tend to value experiences over possessions. I believe that my kids will look back on their lives and remember the things they did more than the stuff they owned. At least that's how it was for me, with the exception of my complete collection of Nancy Drew books. That Carolyn Keene was a wizard. Also, I was today years old when I found out there's no Carolyn Keene and it's a pseudonym for the various authors who wrote the books. Everything is a lie. Anyway, "experiences over possessions" is part of our family's belief system that I hope to pass on to our kids. And now I need Jesus to hold me while I recover from the Carolyn Keene thing.

I still practice my Christian faith, although I've tweaked the method a bit, but after talking with my friends, it seems no matter what faith you grew up in, a lot of us wrestle with what to do. My friend who grew up Hindu wasn't really practicing it when it was just her and her husband, but now that they have a baby, they're starting to think about faith traditions more and we have great conversations about faith and its impact on our family dynamics and raising our kids to believe in something.

I know some people were horribly abused by the churches of their youth, and if that's you, I'm so sorry. I have no words, except that really sucks and I hope the abusers were shut down and not allowed to continue those patterns. I know, based on the news and the stories I hear, that twisted religion is the cause of a lot of the heartache people carry.

I definitely had some baggage that I needed to unpack, but thankfully the majority of my Christian upbringing was a positive one and something I do want to pass on to my kids, while giving them the ultimate freedom to walk away from it in the future. But I hope they develop a faith that guides them and makes them feel loved and like they belong, and if it makes them slightly better members of society and teaches them to maybe give a rip about other people, all the better. After all, the brother of Jesus, James, said that faith without action is dead[17] and that pure religion is caring for orphans and widows,[18] so I'm hoping all this stuff we do will sink in and make them decent human beings.

Sometimes I miss the black-and-white thinking of the way I was raised, but somewhere along the way, I took the red pill when Morpheus offered it and I can't go back. I'm spending my forties peeling away my belief in Jesus from the American Christian culture of my past, and it feels a little like trying to strip wallpaper without damaging the drywall underneath. While I'm having this uncomfortable "come to Jesus" moment, my kids are figuring it out for the first time.

Honestly, you can spend your life beating yourself up about whether or not your kids believe like you do, or you can present your faith to them, answer their questions as best you can, pray for them, and then leave them to figure it out. No amount of spiritual bullying is going to make someone agree with you, and even if that would work, would you want it to? My faith in Jesus is important to me and has impacted who I've become, but quite a bit of that journey took place in my own heart, apart from my parents. They influenced me, for sure, but I had to work it out on my own. I'm still working it out.

As I'm writing this chapter, I'm asking myself why I'm even including faith in the discussion of how to lighten up about parenting. Religion and church have been traditionally the exact opposite, decidedly heavy, even though Jesus said his yoke is easy and his burden is light.[19]

---

17 James 2:17, author paraphrase.
18 James 1:27, author paraphrase.
19 Matthew 11:30, author paraphrase.

The thing is, since my childhood, God has always been my safe place to land. Not the Church, not other Christians, but Christ himself, absolutely. So often I'm able to lighten up about the most difficult challenges because God feels like a safety net in the middle of the chaos. I can bring all my tortured emotions, my anger and pain, and hurl it at God and feel safe doing it, knowing that God isn't going to run away. God isn't freaked out by my disastrous choices or inability to pull myself together. My heavenly parent loves me no matter what.

I want my kids to view me, and ultimately God, the same way. No matter what they throw at me, no matter the choices they make or the crazy shenanigans they get into, no matter how loudly they scream at me or how many times they lose their brand-new shoes, I'll always love them. I'll always be their safe place to land, just like God, only God's way better at it.

God's unrelenting grace and love is the ultimate reason I can lighten up about everything on fire around me. I can't screw up God's love for me. I can keep showing up as my fallible, complicated, snarky self, and God keeps loving me. When things start to feel heavy and impossible, this conviction feels like helium in my veins, lifting me back up and floating me along.

Non-Weird Ways to Incorporate Faith into Family Life

So even though faith is weird and confusing, I want to pass on this legacy of lightness, this glorious grace, to my kids. It's a process. A ridiculous, hilarious process that requires me to lighten up on a regular basis while my kids work this out.

One Sunday morning:

Me: What'd you learn in church today?
Evie: Joseph and the cupburyer to the farrier. (Joseph and
the cupbearer to the Pharaoh.)
Me: So, Joseph's brothers sold him into slavery, and he ended
up in jail with someone who buried cups for a horseshoe
specialist. Got it.

Another Sunday morning:

Alex: What did you learn in church today?
Elliott: They asked us what the happiest place was, and the
answer was supposed to be heaven, but I shouted out
"Netflix!"

One kid thought God was the coolest in preschool, then grew
up a little and wants nothing to do with God talk. That's okay. It's
a long childhood, and let's see where this kid lands. I'm not going
to worry about it. Their journey with religion is like our journeys.
It's complicated and takes a lifetime to sort out.

This kid loves mythology and has no problem believing that
Zeus and Hera are probably a little bit real, but the kid's gonna
need proof when it comes to Jesus. Sure, okay. That's just because
Percy Jackson hasn't gone on a quest with the Apostles John and
Paul to rescue the Holy Hand Grenade. *Indiana Jones and the Last
Crusade* should straighten my kid right out. "You have chosen . . .
wisely."

Adding spiritual formation to the already long list of things
we're supposed to build into our children, alongside putting the

toilet seat down and washing behind their ears, can feel over-whelming. I've learned to calm down about eternity and build daily faith practices into our regular routines. If your faith is important to you, then it's something the kids see you prioritizing in the family schedule. If you're like me, once something's on the calendar or is a habit, then I can relax about it instead of getting to the end of another week and going, "Oh dang it. We forgot to be spiritual again!"

We spend a ton of time in the minivan, so I use car time to pray with my kids. When we're driving by ourselves, I ask them if they need prayer for anything, and then I pray out loud. Now that my kids are older, I have to make them take their earbuds out.

Sometimes we read scripture at the dinner table. I'm too done by bedtime. It blows my mind that we have copies of these ancient writings that have been preserved, translated, and passed down through millennia, so I like to read a chapter, then have a little family discussion about the passage.

I want my kids to learn to read the Bible on their own, so I bribe them. I pay my kids to read the Bible and watch the occasional sermon online. Bible bribery is awesome. I invest my money in things I think are important, and if I think something is important enough to impact my kid, maybe eternally, then I'm willing to ante up. You want that new video game? Read the Book of John and take this quiz. I mean, as long as the information is going in, I'm cool. We don't have to be overly precious about this.

My church is not really into ritual, but I do think kids respond well to the occasional ritual. It's a way to tie their faith to something tangible. Every Christmas Eve and Easter, we do family Communion. I light candles, the kids grab their Bibles, and we gather around the kitchen table. I should mention that typically we have to spend a good half an hour hunting for the kids' Bibles before we start, which shows how often they're reading those things.

I give them scriptures to look up, and they take turns reading them, and then I lead the family in Communion, or the Lord's Supper, or the Eucharist, depending on what brand of Christianity you're familiar with. Or Weird Bread and Wine Thing if your background is something else entirely.

Nothing magical happens, but just a couple times a year—any more would be too much work and I'm not trying to win any awards here—in the middle of holiday chaos, we have this sweet, simple moment to gather as a family and remember the God we worship.

My parents used to do this with me and my brother, and it's the thing I remember most about my religious upbringing. Holy crackers and juice. I don't think there's anything particularly holy about store-brand saltines and some grape juice, but the gathering and remembering—that's where the holy part lies.

When it comes to incorporating faith into your family life, it's okay to ask for help. It's better than okay. We aren't supposed to do this on our own. I get tired and myopic and need wise people helping us. Maybe there's a neighbor or a teacher where you worship who loves your kid. We always hear about praying grandmas. People thank them in awards acceptance speeches, we see them in movies, and I hear of them meeting in church basements. I wonder if the praying grammies are such a force because the parents are too busy keeping everyone alive and trying not to murder everyone. By the time we're all grammies, we're ready to pray. I'm thankful for the praying grandmas and grandpas and promise to pay it forward when I'm empty nesting and can think straight. Till then, my prayers will consist of silent screams and frantic begging.

It's Okay to Doubt

Every summer I send my kids to this Christian camp. It's mostly a great place, and I like that they have college kids who play with them and teach them stuff for a couple of weeks, and I have a whole shelf full of my kids' pottery projects. The only downside is every year I have to undo a few things when they get home.

One of my kids is very logical and practical. This kid wants to see proof, touch it, feel it, smell it. The kid loves science and facts. I love this about my child. One day on the porch, the kid told me one of the camp counselors said you had to choose between science and God. *Hold up. What. No.* I sat up straighter and gripped my coffee cup. Dark roast, give me the strength.

It doesn't have to be either/or. I'm a big fan of both/and when it comes to faith and facts. We had a good conversation about it. Press into science, baby. Enjoy it. Explore and discover. I am 100 percent sure God would want you to learn all you can about the world God created. If you hit a tension, talk to God about it, and it's okay to have that tension. Lighten up about the tension. You can believe in all the scientific systems and that God was present in creation. Don't let some college kid try to pressure you to choose. Don't let anyone. Keep exploring.

I make sure my kids know it's okay to have doubt. Questions are good. Tension is fine. One time my pastor said when we become Christians, we can bring our questions with us. It's not that they go away; they just get smaller.[20] We don't have to resolve all the tension. We can hold space for the tension. So, doubt is wel-

---

20 Andy Stanley, "It's Personal," sermon series from North Point Resources.

come in our home. It's okay if your kids have doubt, and you can, too. You don't have to have an answer for everything. And it's okay to talk about these things. We need to. I don't want to hand my kids a faith they aren't allowed to question.

Growing up, we were taught to stay away from a lot of things. MTV was blocked on our TV. In our small town at the local movie theater, we got two shows at a time that would be there for what felt like months. In junior high we got *Ghost* and I spent every dance swaying back and forth to "Unchained Melody," but I was forbidden from seeing the movie because Whoopi Goldberg played a psychic in it and psychics were outlawed. Every weekend another group of kids would see the movie and I begged and pleaded to no avail. The other movie playing was *Quigley Down Under*, a lesser known work, definitely further down in the canon of early-'90s classics. I called everyone I knew and finally got a couple people to agree to see this second-string movie with me.

My parents have chilled out over the years, and we laugh about these things now, and I respect them for trying their best to do what they heard was right. I'm trying to do the same thing, look at the world around my kids through the lens of my faith, and figure out where the truth lies. It's harder than I thought it would be.

Christianity isn't something I do; it's something that was done for me. I don't have to earn it with good behavior, and what even is good behavior? Because to listen to my kids when they come home from church, it sounds like good behavior is just not swearing. Surely I can teach my kids something more about their faith than avoiding a list of words that some people find objectionable?

These days, I don't have tingly spiritual feelings. I'm pragmatic. Deep in my innermost thoughts, I think the Resurrection really happened. But I'm really tired of the flowery Christianese associated with it. If your kids don't have ooey-gooey feelings about God, that's okay. Pragmatism never hurt anyone. Be honest about your questions, look for ways to show your kids why you believe whatever you do, and you don't have to have an answer for everything. Help them find comfort in the tension. When you think nothing is sinking in, they might surprise you.

Rather than stress about nailing down my kids' belief system by the time they're ten, I try to model my own faith in my daily life without making it oppressive or shoving it down their throats. Every morning I'd come downstairs for breakfast before school and find my dad quietly reading his Bible. He didn't preach out of it or hit me over the head with it. I just saw him reading it a little at the beginning of each day, and now I try to do that with my kids.

My kids see us going to church as a family on Sundays. When we watch a movie, read a book, or meet a friend who holds a different belief system, I explain to my kids the points that are different and the reason I believe what I do, without belittling or judging the other belief system.

I teach them respect and understanding of other people's religions. Our friends invited us to their Hindu blessing ceremony, and my kids sat quietly and listened to their priest and watched what they did. My other friends invite us for their Ethiopian Orthodox feasts celebrating their church holidays. Let your kids see how other families practice faith. We have so much to learn from each other.

Which brings me to an important point about religion. We can believe that our way is the truth while also teaching our kids to respect all religions. We can teach our kids to respect all religions without practicing all religions. We have open conversations about the differences and why we think our way is right, and even the tensions we feel about our way and how our way is maybe getting it wrong, at least in practice. The God part is great, but maybe the people part is lacking, or some might say even a little douchey.

Bad Christian

As your kids get older, they start to compare your family to the families of their friends. You'll send them off to a sleepover and they'll come home with widened perspectives and fresh, new ways to insult you and look down on their own sad family. Usually, my kids relegate these judgments to other people's bigger, better houses, but occasionally they hit deeper.

> **Ana:** Her parents are, like, GOOD Christians.
> **Me:** What's a "good" Christian?
> **Ana:** I don't know.
> **Me:** Well, what's a "bad" Christian?
> **Ana:** You and Dad.

Are we? Is it bad that I'm okay with being bad at this? The thing about us "bad" Christians is the bad part is mostly just cultural and has nothing to do with actual faith in anything.

Am I a bad Christian because I'm ignoring extra rules? Because the way I read the Gospel stories, Jesus was pretty mad at the guys who added extra rules to the faith, and he seemed to free us up from a lot of rules. So, I refuse to win the Christian game by adhering to fake rules, and I don't want my kids to either.

There are plenty of Jesus's actual teachings that Christians suck at. We aren't generous enough. We don't give enough grace. We don't serve the poor and widows. We aren't kind enough to immigrants. Not doing those things makes us actual bad Christians. Getting tattoos and dropping the occasional swear or drinking a scotch aren't really part of it. Focus on what truly matters and lighten up about everything else.

I like incorporating a tangible, practical faith into our home. As often as possible, we serve the community as a family. I want my kids to see me put my money and time where my mouth is. I don't just want to give lip service to this faith thing; I want to put my faith in action by serving others. I try to teach my kids that what we believe should positively impact the people around us. Practically, for our family, this looks like getting together with other families to pack meals at our local food bank, sorting clothes at our county's clothing store for foster families, and sponsoring orphaned and vulnerable children through Children's HopeChest. We teach our kids that God wants us to be generous like Jesus was generous. Maybe if they see us living humbly and giving generously of our time and money, they'll learn to do the same.

On Sunday nights as a kid, my brother and I crowded around our tiny black-and-white portable TV upstairs to watch *In Living Color* while our parents hosted a weekly gathering with other couples in our home. It was like a faith-based book club and prayer meeting, and now Alex and I do the same thing. On Sunday nights, our kids head upstairs while we have neighborhood couples over for our "community group." We talk about everything from parenting and marriage to community service and whose relative needs prayer.

Maybe my favorite part of practicing my belief is the support and friendship of my fellow believers. We cheer for each other's kids and help each other out when we're struggling. Whatever or whomever you believe in, I pray that you'll know the joy of a supportive community, peace of mind, and tremendous hope for your future.

10 WAYS TO GIVE YOUR KIDS A FAITH OF THEIR OWN

1. Make sure they know it's okay to have doubt. Questions are good. Tension is fine.
2. Build faith practices into your regular routines. If your faith is important to you, then it's something they see you prioritizing in the family schedule.
3. Pray in the car.
4. Read scripture at the dinner table.
5. Teach respect and understanding of other people's religions. Let your kids see how other families practice faith.
6. Start early. Teach them from a young age how their faith can guide them. Don't wait till they've fallen apart in high school to mention they could pray about stuff and drag them to church.
7. Model it. They'll do what they see you do.
8. Bribe them. I pay my kid to read the Bible and watch the occasional sermon online. Bible bribery is awesome.
9. Ask for help. Maybe there's a neighbor or a teacher where you worship who loves your kid.
10. Serve as a family. I want my kids to see me put my money and time where my mouth is. I try to teach my kids that what we believe should positively impact the people around us.

16

This Too Shall Pass

Lighten Up About the Future

> "You shouldn't feel so responsible. You tried.
> You did something. That's what counts."
> —*Shaun of the Dead*

Now I've written this whole book, and I don't have any idea how my kids will turn out or if one of them will smother me in my sleep one night in a fit of rage. Someday you could be watching the news and see me on it, going to prison for finally snapping and think, *Didn't I read her book? What a load of crap that was.* Now the pressure's on to get this right.

This is supposed to be the part of the book where I land my plane, assure you that everything's going to be fantastic, and say something saccharine and slightly patronizing like, "You've got this, mama." But how can I know that? I'm not even sure I've got this, much less if you've got this, whatever this is. I told you at the beginning that I shouldn't write this book.

Honestly, no matter what we do, none of us has the assurance that all our kids are going to turn out perfectly, that they're going to tow the company line. And maybe like me, you have a kid or seven or eight with some extenuating circumstances. A diagnosis or two or twenty, maybe some trauma or something out of your hands. Maybe your parenting skills work for five out of six of your kids, your tried-and-true method lands great for your firstborn, but your last one—not so much. Maybe one of your kids is easy and the other one is breaking the mold. Whatever you have going on in your house, I promise you that we don't have it all together in ours.

I don't know how this is going to end up, but no matter what happens with my kids or with yours, I want us to be okay, us parents. Even if we do our best and it all goes to heck, I want us to lighten up and remain mostly calm. Our identity is not wrapped up in however our kids turn out. We can work hard on this parenting gig, but at the end of the day, they'll make their choices and have lives apart from ours.

Can we be okay with that? We'll be happier and have more peace if we figure out now how to parent with open hands, releasing them into the wild blue yonder, feeling satisfaction in doing our part. We can't take credit for their successes, and we can't take blame for their failures. We are separate. But we have a part to play and play it we will.

There's a proverb in the Bible that says, "Start children off on the way they should go, and even when they are old they will not turn from it."[21] Alex's old pastor used to say, "Remember, that's a proverb, not a promise."

So, if in a few years, one of your kids goes off the rails, or one

---

21 Proverbs 22:6 (NIV).

of mine does, or they meet up and go off the rails together, let's stay calm, do what we can, and leave the rest for them to work out themselves, or with God, a good therapist, and maybe a prison warden.

That sounds dire. Hopefully, it won't come to that. But I'm prepared for whatever comes. Some days I'm Maria von Trapp twirling in a sunny field singing about the hills being alive, and other days I'm Jon Snow on top of the wall staring into the icy abyss, muttering, "Winter is coming."

My Kid Stabbed a Kid with a Pencil, and Everyone Lived

You've all heard about *that kid*. You've worried about *that kid* and keeping your kid safe from them. *That kid* is on every bus and at every school at every lunch table. *That kid* might rub off on your kid or teach your kid something bad or be mean to your kid or give your kid a rash or a hickey. Horrible, evil *that kid*.

But what if one day you discover you're *that kid*'s parent?

At some point, most of us will have that kid. Your sweet, beautiful baby will go to school, and one day, you'll get a call or a text or someone angry will approach you at the bus stop or the pool, and you won't be worried about *that kid*, you'll be embarrassed that they live in your house.

Maybe not. Maybe all your babies are precious and would never do anything wrong. For the rest of us, at some point, we're going to be on the wrong side of an incident. I've had several.

Last year, my darling babe stabbed a kid with a pencil on the bus. When the other parent called me, I experienced many emotions. I was horrified and concerned for her injured child. I was embarrassed. And this sick part of me was trying not to laugh. I'm not proud of this part of me. Pencil stabbings are serious business. No one should be stabbing anyone. My child attempted to calm down about something and at that critical moment, lost the battle.

My kid was disciplined. We took it very seriously.

And I had to laugh. Later. By myself. Because sometimes when you step back, kids are crazy, and if we didn't grow up and develop logical reasoning and a smidge of impulse control, we'd do crazy things, too. There are several people I'd like to stab with a pencil right this minute.

I have a lot more serious stories that are not mine to share, but this pencil one seemed small enough that I can tell you. (It wasn't like the icicle scene from *Die Hard 2* or anything. Just a flesh wound. I don't want you to think I'm writing this after visitation at the prison.) Sometimes no matter how much you try to train up a child to make good choices and do the right thing, circumstances or brain chemistry or a series of unfortunate events leads them down a different path, and you get phone calls and have meetings.

Maybe there's no one to blame. Don't beat yourself up about it, unless you've purposely raised a serial killer. Most kids have at least a few issues at some point along the way. Don't let it freak you out. Stay humble, listen, ask questions, believe the best about the other people involved, and figure out what your kid needs to get on track. And someday when your child's the victim, have a little compassion for *that kid* and *that kid*'s parents. Most of us are doing our best. Most of us want everyone to get along. No one is pro–pencil stabbing. (Be sure to check out my next book, *Whittle Your Own Shiv! Crafting Shivs from Basic Household Items*.)

Where Do You Think You're Going?

In an attempt to lower our expectations about parenting and lighten up about all the things we feel we need to accomplish for our families—without giving up entirely and bingeing Netflix with our hand firmly in a bag of Doritos—let's come up with some reasonably attainable goals for the future that we can set. Minimum striving without being a complete amoeba.

At the beginning of each year, we have a family meeting where everyone gets to share ideas for what they'd like to experience and accomplish. If you're the kind of family who loves goal setting, maybe you do this on a weekend away. You bring matching notebooks and break out a new pack of gel pens. That's great for you. Go for it.

For us, as with pretty much everything else, our best time to grab a few decent minutes is around the dinner table. That's because half of us have our mouths full at any given moment, so we're not all scream-talking at each other and there's a chance we might hear each other. Maybe you spread out this conversation and do a series of talks over the course of a week. We only have small snippets of time before the kids rebel and stop listening.

We start with a recap of the previous year. If your kids are like mine, they've already forgotten all the cool stuff you did and think their lives are miserable and clearly our family is poorer and stupider than their friends' families. Remind them about all the stuff.

"We visited the grandparents at the beach, and you had fun at camp, and remember Science Olympiad and how we ate ice cream for dinner sometimes last summer?" Celebrate all the wins and pat yourselves on the back for all that you did and survived.

Then segue into what things you'd like to leave in that year and not do again. Maybe they want a year off from camp, and you need to know this before you pay the hefty registration fee. Or your kid doesn't want to take piano lessons anymore and is trying to get up the courage to tell you. Or everyone is sick of the zoo membership and wants to switch to the science center this year. Take stock of everyone's feelings on the last year, then move on to the next year.

Have someone record everyone's answers in a list. For experiences, maybe someone wants a ski trip. Maybe someone wants to visit the planetarium. Opening weekend tickets to a Marvel movie. Trip to Grandma's. Whatever. At this stage there are no bad ideas. Just communicate to everyone that you can't do all the ideas this year, but you're just getting an idea of what they'd want to do. Maybe everyone gets a realistic one and a shoot-for-the-moon. My kid wants to go to Hawaii as a family. I told her I'm in my forties and have never been to Hawaii, so that's probably not going to happen anytime soon for her. But a girl can dream.

For accomplishments, what's something each person wants to accomplish for the year? On my list this year is finishing this book. (Almost there. I feel like we're near the end? You're ready to be done reading, right? I'm almost done writing.) Maybe for your kid, it's trying out for the soccer team or reading through *The Lord of the Rings* series. Or learning to read. Or learning to read Spanish. I like to focus not only on the results but also the attempts. Trying out for the high school lacrosse team as an eighth-grader and doing your best is still achieving a goal, even if you don't make it. (Ana made it. This is a sports brag. I don't know who I am anymore.)

Trying something is an accomplishment, no matter the results.

I know I sound like one of the Fockers and their Wall of Gaylord, but we celebrate doing our best and trying new things, not just winning. You can't control if the director of the play casts you. But you can control preparing an audition, doing your best, and putting yourself out there.

So, compile your list of everyone's goals for the year, both the things they want to do and the things they want to accomplish, and then you and your partner figure out what works with the calendar and the budget. If your son wants to go scuba diving on an Australian coral reef, maybe that's not attainable, but your local dive center has a class he can take one Saturday.

At your family meeting you can also brainstorm service ideas. For a couple years, our family served every month at our local food bank. Then last year we decided to mix it up and serve at the clothing store for kids in foster care, sorting clothes and preparing hygiene kits. As you think through your year as a family, this is a great time to also think about how your family is going to serve others in your community.

You don't have to look at your family's calendar and plans at the beginning or end of a calendar year. Maybe the beginning of the school year is your time. Maybe you have these talks quarterly. Whatever works for you. But I do think developing the habit of family planning can help you to not drift from year to year.

If we don't consciously steer our families in the direction we want them to go, our environment will do it for us. Whether it's the Joneses, the HGTV family du jour, or your brother-in-law, someone will influence your trajectory. I want to make intentional choices about the time that I have with our kids, and when I know where we're heading on a macro level, it actually helps me lighten up about the little things in between.

If you have a partner, some conversations need to happen between just you two before the kids ever get a peek. A few years ago, Alex and I sat down just the two of us and said, "Okay. We have FIVE SUMMERS before Ana graduates from high school and we can no longer guarantee her presence for family trips. How do we want to spend them?"

That was a wake-up call. She still seemed so tiny. Only five summers left? We made a list of all the camps, activities, and trips we wanted to take with the kids before she took off for the rest of her life. And then we estimated the cost of everything. And that's the moment I realized I could wait on new carpet and would make do with my worn, disgusting sofa for a few more years. Because I value experiences over stuff, and when I saw how much the memories I want to make were going to cost, I realized home improvements could wait awhile longer.

We made a list, things like a road trip to DC to show the kids where we used to live, a visit to Universal Studios to see the Harry Potter world, and even cashing in airplane miles on a trip to London for just me and Alex while the kids were at camp. We tentatively scheduled out which summer would be good for which trips, and we've been slowly working through our list year by year. We space these things out, partially because of budget and time, and partially because of road trip conversations like these:

Kid: Mom! The sun is too bright and it's making it hard to see the TV screen!

Me: Wow, that's rough. When I was a kid, we didn't have TV in the car. We read books, and sometimes I journaled.

Kid: I wanna listen to music.

Me: Sometimes my dad would listen to classical music, or AM talk radio while we sat in silence. So, what I'm saying is I don't feel sorry for you.

Kid: Are we there yet?

Me: We've literally been driving for fifteen minutes.

Kid: Are we out of Georgia yet?

Me: We've been driving for fifteen minutes.

Kid: How much longer?

Me: Please stop talking.

It's a balance. You don't want to obsess so much about the future that you can't enjoy the present. But a little planning keeps life from flying by unchecked.

I thought the preschool years would last forever. It felt like we'd been mounted and preserved under glass and were sitting on God's desk, just a desperate mom shoving writhing kids into car seats while spelling swear words under her breath so they wouldn't repeat them. But then they grew out of the car seats, started school, and life sped up.

I love it. Don't savor every moment of those preschool years. Don't mourn the loss of them. Savor what you can when your kids are little and then strap in because you'll get whiplash going from the kiddie rides to roller coasters. They take off and every week is a blur. Thankfully. If you linger too long in one spot, you can start to chafe. But hang on because before you get a chance to fester, you're on to the next thing. It's wild and wonderful, and the only way we'll survive is if we lighten up.

I say it all the time: the older my kids get, the more I like them. I'm having the best time watching them grow up. The banter around our house makes me laugh on a daily basis, and my kids ask challenging questions and make me think. I give them total credit for developing me into a braver, more honest person who knows who she is. I like who I'm becoming as they become who they are. We are lighter together.

This Too Shall Pass

My dad used to say, "This too shall pass." I'd roll my eyes. *Ugh. Get a new phrase, Dad. Who even says "shall" anymore?*

Last week I caught myself saying it to my kids. This too shall pass. And it will. And the next thing, and the next. That's the perspective of age—what my dad could see and I couldn't all those years ago. That perspective gives us the ability to calm down, because we know that centuries of parents have raised centuries of kids and lived to tell the tale.

Things might be extremely difficult right now. Your kids might be challenging you in ways you never thought possible. Maybe you're encountering new lows and hitting the very limit of what you think you can withstand.

I've been there. Like a second ago. And I'll be there again.

I ran into a friend in line for waffle fries yesterday, and she said, "We need to talk," and it's about things happening with our kids that we can't talk about to just anybody. That's how we keep going, how this too, whatever this is, shall pass. Through relationships. We pick each other up and encourage each other to keep going. We celebrate the wins and mourn the losses together.

The secret is people. Everyday moms and dads locking arms to raise the next generation. Older parents offering wisdom and solace to younger ones. Peers brainstorming solutions. Getting mad together, fighting for, not against, each other.

This too shall pass. It's a blink. It's a moment. Sometimes when I'm ready to quit, I remind myself, *I get to do this*. We get the privilege and responsibility of bringing these baby humans up into adulthood. The audacity. That weirdos like us should do this. Surely there's someone more qualified. Surely someone else could do it better. Maybe. But it's us. So, inhale, exhale, and calm down.

The future is bright, and it'll be here before we know it.

The Lighten Up Guidelines for Laughing at Life

1. We'll let ourselves laugh at our own wonderful weirdness.
I try not to laugh at other people too much (it's a work in progress, people), but I love laughing at myself. I am weird, both accidentally and on purpose, and I'm learning to laugh about it. Embrace your weird side, and if you don't think you have one, look closer. Everybody's got something.

2. We'll engage sweaty subjects with grace and bravery.
Lightening up doesn't mean avoiding serious and important topics. Talking about hard stuff can breathe light and life into relationships rather than stuffing it all down. I want to engage with what people care about. I want to share what I care about. So, let's be brave as we talk about complicated or difficult topics, and let's be gracious and loving with each other as we do it.

3. We'll give ourselves permission to enjoy things in life.
There is no prize for the most stoic, humorless person. It's okay to let ourselves laugh and enjoy the world around us, even in the

middle of hard things. We can let ourselves have fun because we are the boss of ourselves.

4. We'll cultivate homes filled with laughter.

Laughter and lightness are things that you nourish and grow. If you don't tend to them, they wither in the trend toward darkness and solemnity. We need to foster a spirit of fun, model it to our kids, and fill our homes with the freedom to chortle. This means chasing down funny—read funny books, watch funny shows, tell funny jokes, ask funny questions, and let the laughter bubble up.

5. We'll actively look for the silly and ridiculous.

Silly things happen all day long, and we will take the time to notice and savor them. And often ridiculous things that show up to ruin our days would be the very things we'd laugh about if they were happening to our favorite characters on TV. We'll seek to notice the ridiculous, call it what it is, and laugh in the face of it.

6. We'll value storytelling and the people telling the stories.

Everyone has a story, and I want to hear yours. Let's value each other's stories, laugh with each other during the funny parts, empathize with each other during the difficult parts, and listen with both ears, all four heart chambers, and our brain lobes. When we value our stories, we value our humanity.

7. We'll accept that it's okay to suck at some stuff.

We don't have to be great at everything. We'll swim hard in our own lanes and stop trying to take over the whole pool. When we do suck at something, we'll laugh our heads off and embrace the humility and wisdom that comes with beautiful failure.

8. We'll be honest about our feelings and let ourselves feel them.

Some of us are more serious. Some of us are naturally sarcastic or funny. When things happen in our lives, we might feel several emotions all at once, a sad-mad with a side of snort-laugh, maybe a rainbow of happy-embarrassed-nervous. Feelings are complicated, and we all have different combinations at different times. We'll work to acknowledge our feelings, honor the feelings of others, and let ourselves have them.

9. We'll leave space around us for a variety of opinions.

I'm not approachable if I'm taking up all the air in the room. We need to live with plenty of room around us for people to share. We need to learn to listen well and hold space for each other. It's okay to have tension. We don't have to resolve all the tension, but we can learn to live with it kindly and respectfully. We can learn from each other.

10. We'll have fun on purpose because it's important and worthy.

Lightening up is not frivolous or optional. We need to prioritize fun because it's an important part of being human and cultivating relationships with one another. Lightness, playfulness, and humor are worthy pursuits that can help us process difficult topics, traumatic experiences, and the daily rigors of life. We will play together and value that time just as much as we value the serious work.

Acknowledgments

First of all, thanks to everyone in my life who supplied such lovely material for me to write about. All my stories are just that, my stories, and I've endeavored to share them how I remember them. As with all memories, our recollections can be a bit subjective, and if I've erred at all in the retelling, it's a total accident.

Becky Nesbitt and Beth Adams, I knew I wanted you to be mine mine mine from the moment we spoke. I mean, I tried to be cool about it, but I fell in deep, deep like. You guys are hilarious and wonderful, and I'm so grateful for your editorial magic in this book.

It's a dream come true to be at Simon & Schuster. Thanks to Daniella Wexler, Loan Le, and everyone there for your incredible attention to detail and partnership throughout the process. You guys are amazing, and I can't believe I got to work with you on this project.

Kathy Helmers, this is kinda your fault. Thanks for saying, "You know how you said you'd never write a parenting book? I've been thinking about that. What if you did it anyway?" Thanks for letting me ALL CAPS swear-text at you and send you ridiculous photos. Best agent ever.

To our team of wonderful therapists, teachers, and doctors, you make me a better parent. Thanks for your strategies and ideas. You serve our family so well, and I want everyone to have the kind of access and care that we have. You are a gift.

Friends don't let friends parent alone, and I'm grateful for the friends who love me and my kids. Lauren, Chantel, Jenni, Mandi, Chantel, Nichole, Veronica, and Julie, thanks for girls' nights, game nights, and putting up with me. In the event of my premature demise, thanks in advance for deleting all my texts.

Mom and Dad, thanks for raising Nate and me. You did a really great job, because we're terrific, and I think Nate will concur. I find myself asking, "How would Mom and Dad handle this?" when I'm not sure what to do, and usually that gets us where we need to be. You taught me to approach parenting with humility and grace.

Alex, thanks for your excellent partnership, for challenging me, and for serving as head shin guard shover-onner and a one-man IT department for all our family's gadgets. I'm so glad we have each other's backs with these three. Meet me in the basement soon.

Elliott, Evie, and Ana, you guys. I adore you. Thanks for letting me be your mom and for the occasional permission to stick your gorgeous mugs on the interwebz. If you survive your childhood, you're going to make the most amazing adults, and I'm so honored to get a front-row seat. I'm your biggest fan and will continue to scream "I LOVE YOU" in public for the rest of your life, so you can go ahead and give up that fight.